VINTAGE **CLASSICS**

LYDIA GINZBURG

Lydia Yakovlevna Ginzburg was born in Odessa in 1902, and moved to Leningrad in 1922, where she studied at the famous Institute for Art History as a student and later as a colleague of Victor Shklovsky, Yury Tynianov and Boris Eikhenbaum, the major figures of Russian Formalism. She survived the purges, the 900-day siege of Leningrad and the anti-Semitic campaigns that followed the war to become, in the 1960s to 1980s, a friend and inspiration to a younger generation of Petersburg literary scholars and poets, including Alexander Kushner and Elena Shvarts. She was a prominent cultural figure in the years of perestroika, when she began to publish notes and essays that she had been writing for the 'desk drawer' starting in the 1920s. Her books include venerated works of literary scholarship such as *On Lyric Poetry*, *On Psychological Prose* (published in the English translation by Princeton University Press) and *On the Literary Hero*. The collection of her prose that appeared in her lifetime, *Person at a Writing Table* (1989), and which contained *Notes from the Blockade*, as well as posthumous editions have established Ginzburg as the innovative author of what she called 'in-between' genres – notes, essays and fragmentary narratives – that describe and analyse the human experience of a historically catastrophic era spanning much of the twentieth century. Lydia Ginzburg died in 1990.

LYDIA GINZBURG

Notes from the Blockade

TRANSLATED FROM THE RUSSIAN BY
Alan Myers

AND

A Story of Pity and Cruelty

TRANSLATED FROM THE RUSSIAN BY
Angela Livingstone

BOTH TEXTS EDITED BY
Emily Van Buskirk

VINTAGE

1 3 5 7 9 10 8 6 4 2

Vintage
20 Vauxhall Bridge Road,
London SW1V 2SA

Vintage Classics is part of the Penguin Random House
group of companies whose addresses can be found at
global.penguinrandomhouse.com

Penguin
Random House
UK

Notes from the Blockade first published in *Neva*, Leningrad, 1984
Subsequently published by Sovetskii pisatel' in
Chelovek za pismennym stolom, Leningrad, 1989
First published in Great Britain by The Harvill Press in 1995
This edition revised by Emily Van Buskirk first published by
Vintage Classics in 2016

A CIP catalogue record for this book is available
from the British Library

ISBN 9780099583387

Typeset in India by Thomson Digital Pvt Ltd, Noida, Delhi

Printed in Great Britain by Clays Ltd, St Ives plc

Penguin Random House is committed to a sustainable future
for our business, our readers and our planet. This book is made
from Forest Stewardship Council® certified paper.

Contents

Note on the translation ix

NOTES FROM THE BLOCKADE xiii

Around *Notes from the Blockade*
 Notes during the Siege 81
 Paralysis 98
 Excerpts from a Siege Day 106

Draft "Theoretical Section" of the Manuscript
"Otter's Day" (Excerpts) 117

Preface to "A Story of Pity and Cruelty" 129

A STORY OF PITY AND CRUELTY 135

'Speaking Directly About Life':
 Introduction to the 1995 Harvill edition
 by Alexander Kushner 211

Contents

Note on the Translation ix

NOTES FROM THE UNDERGROUND iii

A ... Satire on Human Nature
Notes during the Siege 41
Parables 99
... the ... Stage Do ... 105

That "Diabolical Self-love" of the Masochist:
"Otherness" ... Interpreted 117

Parables on A Story of Joy and Cruelty 127

A STORY OF JOY AND CRUELTY 145

Speaking Directly About Life:
Introduction to the 1995 Hartsill edition
by Alexander Knabine 241

Note on the translation

The current edition is a modified version of the Alan Myers translation, published in 1995 under the title *Blockade Diary*. The changes aim to bring the text closer into agreement with Lydia Ginzburg's style, and to clarify her meaning when necessary. The new title, *Notes from the Blockade*, more closely reflects the original, *Notes of a Blockade Person* (*Zapiski blokadnogo cheloveka*). Diary-writing was a common activity among citizens of Leningrad enduring the blockade, and yet Ginzburg did not write diaries. Her essayistic work of documentary prose is written in the third person, and resembles "notes" in its fragmentary and heterogeneous structure. Her title echoes Dostoevsky's *Notes from Underground*, another philosophical text in the Petersburg–Leningrad tradition, which explores the contradictions and travails of a person's life in the northern capital.

For a long time, readers were left to guess at when and how Ginzburg wrote this text. For example, she appended a triple date to the work – 1942–1962–1983 – but did this represent three distinct stages of composition, highpoints in the process, or were the dates altogether symbolic? If she completed the work in stages, which parts were written when, how much of the original manuscript remained or was removed, and how significant were the revisions? Research at Ginzburg's archives (held at the Manuscripts Division of the Russian National Library in St Petersburg, Russia, Fund 1377) recently revealed that she in fact drafted the majority of what became *Notes from the Blockade* in the war years, most intensively in 1943–4. Her blockade-era manuscripts

include a narrative describing, in detail, a single representative siege day (structured in three parts: the morning chores before work; the work day; the evening after work). There is also a sketch that became "Paralysis"; records and analysis of conversations in bread lines, bomb shelters, the Writers' Cafeteria and the radio station; philosophical and historical reflections on the effects of the war on the attitudes and morals of her generation. Lydia Ginzburg was extremely active as a desk-drawer writer during the war years, and in addition to these texts that made their way into *Notes of a Blockade Person*, she wrote other notes, essays, sketches, and a longer narrative ("A Story of Pity and Cruelty") that she left unpublished. These writings from the archives, as well as earlier drafts of *Notes of a Blockade Person*, have been published in the Russian edition *Passing Characters. Notes of a Blockade Person. Prose from the War Years*, edited by Emily Van Buskirk and Andrei Zorin (Moscow: Novoe izdatel'stvo, 2011).

It is unclear when the author halted her work on *Notes of a Blockade Person*. However, it appears in the years following the war and until Stalin's death (1946–53), Ginzburg even ceased writing essays and notebooks altogether (otherwise a continuous occupation from 1925–90). It seems that she resumed work on her blockade prose in 1962, probably in connection with the second wave of the thaw, which had made possible the publication of Alexander Solzhenitsyn's *One Day in the Life of Ivan Denisovich*. Ginzburg moved away from the "day in the life" structure, and it can be surmised that she did so in order to distance herself from Solzhenitsyn's famous work. Other modifications included a change of the hero's name (from Otter to the more anonymous N) and the drafting of a "Preamble" out of an unfinished blockade-era theoretical essay. Ginzburg made some further revisions in the 1970s, and then as she prepared the text for publication in a 1984 edition of the journal *Neva*, she again made modifications – cutting

and pasting (as we would say now), and also simply cutting some sections. She revised the text once more for a republication in one of her books in 1987; she included some earlier cut sections in "Around *Notes from the Blockade*" (1989) and "*Notes from the Blockade*: Part II" (1991), which consists of conversations (transcribed by Ginzburg in 1942–3) at the radio station and at the Writers' Cafeteria, along with analysis of these conversations (resembling the conversations in the bread line and bomb shelter on pages 45–7 of this edition).

Emily Van Buskirk, 2016

Notes from the
Blockade

During the war years, people used to read *War and Peace* avidly, comparing their own behaviour with it (not the other way round – no one doubted the adequacy of Tolstoy's response to life). Readers would say to themselves: right, I've got the proper feeling about this. So then, this is how it should be. Whoever had energy enough to read, used to read *War and Peace* avidly in besieged Leningrad.

Tolstoy had said the last word as regards courage, about people doing their bit in a people's war. He also spoke of how those caught up in this common cause continued playing their part involuntarily, while ostensibly busy solving problems affecting their own lives. The people of besieged Leningrad worked (while they could) and saved (if they could) both themselves and their loved ones from dying of hunger.

And in the final reckoning that was also essential to the war effort, because a living city barred the path of an enemy who wanted to kill it.

Something of this is related here.

I not only had to show the siege life that was common to all, but also the day-to-day existence of one person. This

person is a fictional* composite (which is why he is called N†), an intellectual in exceptional circumstances.

It was a day in the Leningrad spring of 1942, though the word "spring" had an odd ring to it. The bread ration had been increased, trams made their diffident way along frozen streets. The Germans had halted the bombing raids, but were shelling the city several times each day. The strongest and most vital people had already died – or had survived. The feeble went on dying more slowly. The word "spring" had an odd ring to it.

N wakes up, a blockade person‡, exempt from call up because of defective eyesight. The previous summer he had

* The Russian word Ginzburg uses, *uslovnyi*, can mean either "fictional" or "conventional", as in "according to literary convention". Another definition would be "conditional" (as in an experiment).

† The use of the Roman letter N, rather than its Cyrillic equivalent, to denote an unidentified location or person has always been the convention in Russian literature. Its associations with Russian terms like "nobody" and "a certain . . ." make it appropriate to use the letter for a composite human being. Instead of the Roman letter N, however, Ginzburg spells out the word "En" in Cyrillic (Эн), which almost approximates a proper name. In the wartime drafts for this narrative (as well as other prose narratives of this period of her creativity), the hero's name was Otter, which stood for "other" (*l'autre*) and "author" (*auteur*).

‡ "Blockade person/person of the blockade": N, the persona described by Lydia Ginzburg as typifying siege behaviour, is male, but is often replaced as a narrative focalizer by the more generalized, and gender-neutral "blockade person". The word "person", while not gender-specific in Russian, is grammatically masculine and therefore takes masculine pronouns (he, his), verb endings and adjectives. Here we preserve these masculine personal pronouns (he, his instead of their or his/her) in connection with the blockade person for historical accuracy and to retain the effect that is achieved in Ginzburg's text: seamless transitions between "N" and the "blockade person". In her semi-fictional, semi-autobiographical narratives, Ginzburg followed the Russian literary tradition (patriarchal of course) of representing typical experiences through (grammatically and often superficially) male characters.

2

been accustomed to waking up in a different manner – always on the dot of six, to the sound of the communal radio in the corridor. Then he had developed a habit of waking ten or fifteen minutes earlier and lying there, listening. After a minute or two, he couldn't stand it and went out into the corridor in his pyjamas. His neighbours were already standing there half-dressed, their faces tense and eager. The feeling was that if the announcer's usual unnatural voice started listing radio stations, it meant that nothing out of the ordinary had happened that day . . . N knew this way of thinking was an aberration but he couldn't break himself of the habit. Things didn't start with the announcer, however; first there came a series of brief little rings and pauses, making up a sound pattern. Never had we heard such a dismal sound. Then followed the listing of radio stations with its false hint at a stable situation. Finally there came the terribly brief information bulletin (they seemed to get shorter and shorter) which consisted in those days of directions of the German advance. And people stood by the radio with fainting hearts, taking in the latest direction. The newsreader used to speak with unnatural slowness. You could count the seconds separating each word, each centre of population. The direction from what they asked . . . people knew. Next it would be Luga, then . . . That's how it was in the summer of 1941.

There was a terrible thirst for information. Five times a day people would drop whatever they were doing and run to the loudspeaker. They used to fall on anyone who had been as much as a yard nearer the front line than they had, or to the authorities, or to any source of information. Those interrogated used to get annoyed at the stupid questioning, because what those who were asking wanted to know was something altogether different from what they asked. They wanted to know what it was like, the war, how it was going to be . . .

This dearth of information was a marked feature of those first days, mingling strangely with the extensive preparation,

the years-long instilling of the idea of the inevitability and crushing totality of the event.

Everyone who lived through it remembers their own first day of the war. Sunday. A small queue at the suburban ticket office. Your hand taking the change and the rectangular cardboard ticket. And at that precise instant a voice, seemingly astonished (or was it?): "It's Molotov* speaking . . . He's saying something about . . ."

By this time people had crowded round the station entrance. Words were issuing from the loudspeaker and each one, independently of its meaning, was a separate container of the agony that lay ahead, a vast, all-encompassing agony. The speech ended. I went back home, the ticket painfully crushed into my palm. That night they would wait a long time for me on the platform down there, and wait in vain. Less than half an hour had passed and we were already being borne away inexorably from our pre-war emotional cast of mind.

I returned home along streets apparently still pre-war, and past objects still pre-war but whose significance was now altered. There was as yet no suffering, no mortal anguish, no terror; on the contrary, there was an excitement – and a feeling bordering on levity that this life was coming to an end.

In this first instant of the event which was coming to pass, it seemed that one ought to be rushing off somewhere, that nothing could now be as it had been before. Then it turned out that, for the moment, a great deal was as it had been before. The trams were still running, royalties were being paid, the usual things were on sale in the shops. It was astonishing. The sense of a former life coming to an end had been so unbearably intense to begin with that the mind, setting all intermediate events to one side, concentrated exclusively on the denouement. In these unheard-of circumstances, it

* Vyacheslav Mikhailovich Molotov (1890–1981): close associate of Stalin and Minister for Foreign Affairs, 1939–49 and 1953–6.

did not wish to run around in circles; it wanted to be stern and steadfast. The least-prepared found no other way to do it than to start at the end and come to terms with their own personal destruction. They used to say to each other quite sincerely: "Well, in all this uncertainty the one clear thing is – we're done for." For about a fortnight it seemed to them that this course was the simplest, and that they were facing up to it pretty calmly. Later on it became clear that dying was harder than it seemed at first sight, and with an effort, bit by bit, they wrenched their lives away from dystrophy*, and many of them, consciously or not, did their bit for the common purpose.

Later, people began listening to the loudspeaker in a different fashion, more as a routine. The sense that what was a historical, epochal event was at the same time intensely personal (the loudspeaker prophesying each one's fate) withered away. This cup did not pass from anyone, and everybody realized that this was the way war was. A new reality came into being, unprecedented, but still resembling the former one more than seemed possible. It had to be made sense of. People felt now that their fate depended not on the newsreader's formulae, but on factors a great deal smaller in scale and closer at hand: the occupation of point N, a battery established in Ligov, the breakthrough of a barge-load of grain. By winter indeed, waking up in the morning only meant being linked into a series of constantly renewed miseries, lasting until sleep came again.

* A medical term, translating the Russian *distrofiia*. *Distrofiia* was coined by Leningrad's medical community to refer to starvation as a deadly disease, and was widely adopted by Leningraders during the blockade. The euphemism diverted responsibility from the state for the death of the citizenry. Thus, while in English the word is most commonly used in phrases such as "muscular dystrophy", Ginzburg uses it for the extreme weakness and wasting away of body and mind that are caused by chronic lack of food.

Remarque constructed his novel around the bulletin which announced: *All Quiet on the Western Front* on the very day his hero was killed on that front. It was a typical manifestation of the individualist pacifism that became the reaction to the First World War. People of those years (especially westerners) did not wish to understand that social life is a mutual social guarantee (otherwise it is merely brute force and oppression). We, on the other hand, knew that on the day when any one of us was killed by Hitlerite shrapnel – it would be announced somewhere that: "Under enemy shelling, Leningrad carried on with its normal working and business life". But at the same time, everybody here would say: *We* have surrounded Kharkov, *we* have taken Oryol . . . The troops have penetrated, consolidated, advanced . . . Behind the formulae summarizing these actions lay the thousands of individual people who took part in them, perished and did not live to reap the fruits. And behind them were still millions more who did not take part, but would reap the fruits. What had this to do with those who perished and what did they need it for? Nothing. Nothing, of course. It's only from the religious point of view that the dead can need anything. But the living do have their needs. The living are nourished by blood. Some as parasites, others like honoured guests at the feast, responding with an offering of their own blood. The sense of inferiority among those who decline is suppressed neither by their self-interested arguments, nor by their notion that they are of more use elsewhere, nor by their assertion of their own status among the creative elect. It does not do to think though, that those who understood the laws of human connectedness were released from the practice of selfishness, or that it triumphantly led them into a heroic perception of life. For those who were unprepared, these laws remained terrible and theoretically beyond their strength.

In the circumstances of the siege, the first and closest degree of the social guarantee was the family, the cell

of blood and daily life with its inexorable demands for sacrifice. People will say: the ties of love and blood make sacrifice easier. No, it's much more complicated than that. So painful, so fearful was it to touch one another, that in propinquity, at close quarters, it was hard to distinguish love from hatred – towards those one couldn't leave. One couldn't leave – but one *could* offend, hurt someone's pride. And so the nexus was maintained. Every possible relationship – comradeship, discipleship, friendship, love – fell away like leaves; that one remained in force. Writhing with pity or cursing, people shared their bread. Cursing they shared it, and sharing, they died. Those who departed from the city abandoned these domestic sacrifices to those left behind. And the inadequacy of the sacrifice too (I survived – that means I didn't sacrifice enough), and along with the inadequacy, remorse.

Now it was the beginning of summer. A benign summer, not too hot. Waking up every morning, N felt an astonishing absence of suffering, something he had still not got used to. It was the first impression of the day – and the best. Legs and arms lay quietly on the sofa, itself smooth and soft enough. The window was open. He was neither cold nor hot. It was light all around. And it would stay light, the whole of the white night through. He didn't even feel like eating. That was about to become a matter of pressing concern, however – it was always present somewhere (like love in a lover), but for the moment he didn't have to think about it. N threw back the sheet and exposed his body to the light, bright air, neither cold nor hot.

But N knew that he had only to turn onto his left side and he would see the chaos that lay in wait for him (in those days, those working in the humanities didn't yet analyse things in terms of organization, information and entropy). The everyday turmoil – a plate with cigarette stubs, jetsam from the depths of chaos, a jacket on the case of a silenced

typewriter. Why? Because a helpless tremor of exasperation had seized an exhausted man and he had been unable to carry his jacket to a more suitable place. Altogether things had slid down from their allotted places, they were blurred, boundaries flowed into formlessness. Only the greying books stood in a strange dead orderliness on the wall-mounted shelves. Things had partially recovered their significance after all. Not like it had been in the winter . . .

A hostile world was on the offensive and pushing its outposts forward. The closest of these outposts had suddenly turned out to be one's own body. Now there was a "breathing space"*, but during the winter it had been a constant source of potential misery – with all its new ribs and angles, especially terrifying for those inclined to stoutness and who relied on a milk-and-apples diet (once a week) to counter it. In the winter, while people were discovering bone after bone, the alienation of the body proceeded, the splitting of the conscious will from the body, as from a manifestation of the hostile world outside. The body was emitting novel sensations, not its own. If a person went upstairs (with difficulty and an accompanying novel feeling of agonizing fleshlessness) or bent down to look for his galoshes or tried wriggling into the sleeves of his overcoat – the sensations were alien, as if they were being experienced by someone else altogether. As exhaustion grew, the alienation intensified. At length everything split apart in an odd way – an emaciated envelope in the category belonging to the hostile world, and a soul located separately, somewhere inside the ribcage. A graphic embodiment of philosophical dualism.

During the period of greatest exhaustion everything became clear: the mind was hauling the body along with it.

*　Reference to summer 1942 when conditions were far better than in the freezing winter: the double quotation marks distinguish its special meaning. The same word (*peredyshka*) in other contexts is not given quotation marks and is sometimes rendered as "respite".

The automatism of movement, its reflex nature, its age-old correlation with the mental impulse – all that was gone. It turned out, for example, that the vertical posture was by no means inherent in the body; the conscious will had to hold the body under control, otherwise it would slither away as if it were falling down a cliff. The will had to lift it up and sit it down or lead it from object to object. On the worst days it was not only difficult climbing stairs, it was very hard to walk on level ground. And now the will was becoming involved in things it had not been concerned with since it was born. "See, I'm walking along," it says, "that is, I really mean my body is walking and I have to keep a sharp eye on it. Let's say I move my right leg forward, the left one moves back, pivots on its toes and bends at the knee (how poorly it manages that!), then it pulls itself off the ground and moves forward through the air, then lowers itself, as the right leg contrives to move back. Hell knows! You have to watch the way it goes back, otherwise you could fall over." It was the most ghastly dancing lesson.

Even more insulting in its abruptness was losing one's balance. It wasn't weakness, not staggering out of weakness, it was something else altogether. A person wants to place his foot on the edge of a chair, to tie his shoelaces; he loses his balance at that very moment, with a thudding in his temples and a sinking heart. The body has just slithered out of control and wants to fall like an empty sack into some incomprehensible abyss.

A whole series of foul processes is going on inside the alienated body – a degeneration, a drying-out, a swelling up, not like a good old-fashioned illness, because it's being carried out on seemingly moribund material. Some of these processes were even imperceptible to the person stricken by them. "But he's already swelling up, isn't he," they say about him – but he doesn't know about it yet. For a long time people didn't know whether they were swelling up or putting on weight.

Suddenly a person starts to be aware that his gums are swelling. He feels them with his tongue, terrified, then prods them with his finger. He can't leave them alone, especially at night. He lies there with an intense feeling of something hardened and slippery, its painlessness especially fearful: a layer of non-living tissue in his mouth.

For months on end people – the greater part of the citizens – used to sleep without undressing. They lost sight of their body. It disappeared into an abyss, immured in clothing, and there in the depths it changed and degenerated. A person knew it was turning into something horrible. He wanted to forget that somewhere far away, under the quilted jacket, under the sweater, under the vest, under the felt boots and the puttees, he had an unclean body. But the body advertised its presence through pain and itching. The most resilient people washed themselves sometimes and changed their underclothes. Then an encounter with the body could not be avoided. They would examine it with grim curiosity, conquering their desire to remain ignorant. It was unfamiliar, with new hollows and angles every time, bruised and rough. The skin was a blotchy sack, too big for its contents.

Now the body was coming up to the surface again. It wallowed in the air, breathing. It was indeed a breathing space for everyone.

Generally speaking, everything now consisted of three intersecting planes. Somewhere in the irrecoverable distance glimmered that former life . . . It had seemed to us extremely badly organized, when we had been living it; now it was like a fairy tale: water in the taps, light at the press of a switch, food to buy in the shops . . . There existed memory and the inertia of winter . . . There existed the "breathing space". The "breathing space" was sad and edgy in its fragility.

Things and gestures intersected, belonging as they did to different planes. From that former life there was the engraving

above the bookshelf and a Crimean clay jug on the shelf – a present. The woman who had given it was now in unoccupied Russia and the remembrance of her had become a pale and unnecessary thing for N. That winter in the enveloping chaos it seemed that the vase and even the bookshelves were something in the nature of the Pogankino Palace* or the ruins of the Colosseum, in that now they would never have any practical significance again (that's why it cost him no pang to break them apart and chop them up). Later on, things began slowly to return to their significance. N got used to that, also slowly and mistrustfully. It was like taking off a pair of felt boots. N never took his boots off; he somehow imagined that felt boots were by now an essential attribute of a human being. He wore them till the slush came, till it was impossible to go on with them. And then he swapped the battered toil-worn boots for a pair that was hardly worn and had the fresh creak of shoes. Nobody around thought this at all surprising for some reason. But for N it was a strange and important fact – a discovered opportunity to return their original meaning to objects. He had scarcely read anything yet, but now the shelves rising above the chaos of scattered chairs, above the full and empty tins on the edge of his writing desk, were suggesting they should carry out their function once more. And the automatic gesture with which N wound up his alarm and put it on the chair next to his sofa (this clock hadn't worked during the winter, the mechanism had frozen) belonged altogether to the former life. On the other hand, the haste with which everyone threw off every last stitch when they went to bed – that belonged to the "breathing space". It had all the avidity and edginess of a temporary state before a second winter came, which no one was brave enough to

* A historical and architectural landmark in Pskov, built in the seventeenth century and once belonging to the tradesman Sergei Ivanovich Pogankin.

think about; behind that attitude lay the winter trauma of unremoved clothing.*

Without fail, once you got up you had to go to the window. The age-old unchanging morning gesture of renewing your links with the world. In the background, trees rising above the lattice of the square, the tram stop at the bend, now heaped up with bricks and beams. The tram stop had a new sound these days. The tumbled beams thumped like a shell-burst; the freight trams going round the curve wailed like an anti-aircraft siren. The people by the stop looked small from here and very much in a hurry. They were like a swarm of schoolboys coming out of school. It was astonishing to think there might be professors among them, doctors, regarded timidly by their patients, officials.

A year before, the age-old morning view from the window had taken on a new meaning – it had become a question addressed to the world, one expecting an answer. These days the world might have anything you like in store, up to and including the very worst; one needed as many witnesses as possible to the continuing flow of things. The trams were re-assuring, like the voice of the newsreader, who had announced the radio stations. A centre existed, invisibly directing the

* In earlier drafts (starting with the blockade-era manuscript "Otter's Day") there follows a long passage on body lice, which was most likely removed for reasons of censorship in the first 1984 publication, and then never restored by the author, even as censorship restrictions loosened. The passage analyzes why body lice (compared to worms, spiders, fleas and bedbugs) inspired a particular, irrational horror – for example, because of their transparency (which "laid bare the device", a play on formalist literary theories) and hypnotic immobility. Ginzburg summarizes that it was "more difficult to grow accustomed to body lice than to carrying buckets up six floors, or to bombardments". And she notes that obsession with lice started after the great hunger and cold – at the end of winter, "when people began to recover, when people gradually started to undress".

12

red tramcars. The cars ran, the centre functioned. The rails flowed out and fell back into it. Every tram was centrally controlled, attached to the system by its trolley. Moving his curtain aside, N watched in relief as the battered red tram creaked round the corner, obedient to the centre, bound to its rails, linked by its trolley-arm.

In this morning hour of renewing relationships, the world stood clearly revealed in its dual function – hostile and protective. The things which crushed and harassed, poisoned and burned – these were also the things which served as a defence or a substitute for evil. They served as a physical defence, and the last refuge and shelter amid the fear of internal isolation.

This had been the world one year before, on first looking through the window. Then followed the long months when the world went away from the ice-sheathed windows.

There was no peace whatever that winter. Even during the night. One might have thought that the body would relax at night. But as a matter of fact the struggle for warmth continued even in sleep. It wasn't always because people were cold – they piled too many things on themselves for that. But this was the reason why the body continued to struggle. The bedclothes weighed heavily, and what was worse, they kept slipping and crawling off in all directions. To hold onto the pile, you had to apply barely noticeable but eventually fatiguing muscular efforts. You had to learn to sleep motionless, neatly disposed, with a special knack of curling your leg to anchor the foundation of the construction. Otherwise the whole lot could slip to the floor in one go with implacable cruelty. And then, in the dark, in the murderous cold, you would have to pile the edifice up again, by now hopelessly unstable and useless. You couldn't spread your arms or raise your knees even a little under the blanket or turn suddenly to press your face into the pillow. All of which is to say that neither body nor nerves were ever fully rested.

In their apartments people battled for life, like perishing polar explorers. In the morning they would wake up in a bag or a cave constructed since the evening before out of all the things they had managed to drag over themselves. They would wake up at four o'clock or five. Overnight they had contrived to get warm. But the cold that was to torment them unceasingly through the day lay all around. Nevertheless, people waited eagerly – not for morning because morning in the sense of light came much later – no, they were waiting for an excuse to get up, as the start of a new day drew nearer, that is, six o'clock, when the shops and bakeries opened. Which is not to say that people always set off for the bread shop at six. On the contrary, many tried to spin out the bread-collecting business (as far as their strength permitted). But six o'clock was a consoling frontier bringing the awareness of new possibilities. In its own way this was the best moment of all – the bread was all to come, but it was an attainable reality of the coming day. The impatience of hunger overcame the fear of the cold. It drove people from caves warmed by their breath out into the frost of their own room. Getting up was easy, easier than in the former life, when fried eggs were waiting, and didn't need thinking about. The transition was simpler now as well. People slept almost without undressing; it was enough just to stick your legs quickly into the boots which stood by the bed.

A typical siege day would begin with a man going out into the kitchen or onto the dark staircase to chop the daily ration of splinters and small pieces of wood for the little stove. The night had hardly begun to disperse and through the shattered glass of the staircase window, the walls of the houses opposite looked dark, not yellow. The chopping had to be done by feel, guiding the slanted axe into the log, then letting fly. One's hands were in a very bad state. The fingers tended to double up and freeze in some chance attitude and the hand would lose its ability to grasp. Then it could only be used as a

14

paw, like a stump or a club-like implement. A person would scrabble about in the darkness and scrape together the chips which had scattered across the stone landing, grip the heap of chips between his two stumps and throw them into the basket.

Then he would still have to fetch water from the frozen cellar. An icy layer covered the steps of the communal laundry, and people came down this declivity on their haunches. And went back upstairs placing the bucket in front of them, looking for a suitable lodging point in the ice. In its own way it was a mountain climb.

The resistance of every object had to be overcome through one's own will and body without the intervention of technical aids. A man would descend the stairs with empty buckets and through the shattered window in front of him lay the narrowing expanse of the yard which he would have to negotiate with full buckets. This abrupt awareness of space, its physical reality, brought on a feeling of despondency. It was odd the way this water dragged the hands and shoulders down like a stone, crushing a man into the ground (it was odd anyway that colourless, swift-flowing water could be as heavy as stone) – the very stuff that ran so easily up the pipes, storey after storey. A waterpipe is a human concept, a linkage of things which overcomes chaos, a sacred organization, a centralization. The friendly side of a two-faced world turned towards man. But technology – the linking of things, is a reciprocal concept. The world which grants the technology wants your life – in exchange for running water and the light you can turn on at the flick of a switch.

With full buckets you can rest on the bottom steps. Head thrown back, you measure the height before you. In the far distance there is a ceiling with a sort of alabaster moulding. This moulding comes just in the middle of a right-angle dangling zigzag in the staircase. It turns out the staircases actually are suspended in the air (if you look closely it's really frightening), held in place by some invisible interior

15

connection with the house. Throwing your head back, you measure the towering staircase space you will have to cross using willpower and your own body to ferry that water, bearing down like a stone.

Throughout the day, there are many more spaces still to traverse – chiefly the one separating you from dinner. After all, it's better to dine in one of the official departmental canteens, where the porridge is more like porridge. N runs off to lunch through the freezing cold, through the mockingly beautiful city, crunching through the frost. Alongside him and towards him run (or crawl, there's no middle way) people with briefcases, string bags and lunch pails tied to the end of club-like arms. People run through the frost, over-coming the now tangible space. The more intellectual of them recall Dante as they do so, that circle of Dante's Hell where cold reigns. In the canteen it will be just as cold, so that the fingers won't straighten out after being outside and the spoon has to be jammed between the thumb (the only active digit) and the frozen stump.

Lunch itself also represents the conquest of space; small spaces agonisingly crammed with queues. The queue in front of the door, the queue to the controller; the queue for a place at the table. Lunch, a momentary and ephemeral affair (a plate of soup, so many grams of porridge) was given exagger-ated importance and slowed down, according to the classical laws of composition. People are asked what they are doing and they answer: having lunch.

There was a period of constantly repeated air raids. On the way to lunch you had to sit them out in a cellar or make your way through a barrage of anti-aircraft guns and police whistles. And people detested the policemen who saved them from the bombing, whereas they accepted the bombing as an obstacle on the way to lunch. Some people used to set off for lunch at eleven in the morning (that was usually a quiet time) and come back about six or seven.

Some used to bring something back with them for the people at home (if they still had any). It was totally dark at home. They would stoke up the little stove and in its smoky light they would pour the soup from the tin they had brought into a pan, meanwhile cutting 40 grams of bread into slices. Then the one who had come in from dining in the outside world would draw close up to the smoking, flaring stove to warm his hands. And as long as the daily ration of wood splinters lasted, there was no tearing him away from this enjoyment. In the room behind his back lay fog and raging cold. There was only a little circle of light and heat outlined round the stove door. The circle of life. The only thing you could really get warm were the palms of your outthrust hands. They absorbed the fire that played about them. It was a measureless enjoyment, only marred by the fact that the daily ration of wood was irrevocably becoming exhausted.

It was that very expectation of an end, the awareness of the inexorable depletion of our vitality which poisoned every joy and the very sense of life itself. The circumstances of the siege made that formula glaringly obvious. They made it glaringly obvious that the endlessly renewed achievement of endlessly shattered goals was no more than running round a closed circle.

What efforts were required to drive a man from one agonizing action to another? No, no particular psychological efforts were needed. Every misery – food pails in the frost, buckets on the stairs – was a release from worse suffering, a substitute for evil. A drowning person who still struggles doesn't grudge that struggle, it's not unpleasant to struggle. It is the suppression of one sort of suffering by another, it is the crazed driving urgency of the wretched, which explains (a phenomenon poorly understood by the well-fed individual) why people can live in isolation, in a convict prison, in the last degree of poverty or humiliation, while their fellow human beings in cosy cottages put a bullet through their temple for

no apparent reason. Suffering continually strives to be rid of itself, with the aid of different, surrogate suffering. The aims, interests and impulses of suffering give rise to whole series of fixed actions, constantly self-renewing and no longer burdensome to the will. But the will is powerless to disrupt this sequence in order to introduce some new gesture unfortified by suffering. Thus was the circle of the winter siege day laid down. During the breathing space too, this movement, circular and indissoluble still goes on, gradually subsiding. People bear this movement within them, like a wound.

Now, during the breathing space, when the impulses of suffering are not so overpowering and compelling, the daily round demands even more mental effort. On the other hand, we do not make convulsive movements at random as we seek out particles of food, light or warmth. Our running in circles takes on the nature of a regular routine to some extent. For many people a regimen, a work routine was always an unattainable dream. The effort to set their life in order just wouldn't come. Now life has been swept clear of any kind of idle chatter, all those substitutes and mystifications, lovers' misunderstandings or the demands of a second or third profession, the exhausting vanity which drove people on to where they shouldn't be at all – it was where their friends and coevals had reached, and that naturally gave them no peace. We, who had lost so much time, had suddenly been given time, empty, but not free.

N had also dreamed of a working routine all his life and considered that he had not achieved it only because of his habit of getting up late (it's a habit of Leningraders if they don't have to go to work early). Everything always started from the fact that the morning had gone and that wonderful feeling of the unbroken fullness of the day ahead was irretrievably spoiled. As it was all spoiled in any case, N used to let himself go with relief and things took their course as usual. Now, however, the cause and effect connection of impulses and

18

actions had been crudely exposed and screwed into place. Now he woke at six because, like everybody else in the city (who wasn't on duty), he went to bed early and got up at once in the morning because he was hungry or was afraid that he was going to be. He performed the domestic chores in the morning – not to do them, to put them off would have been like death. He went to the editorial office where he worked, since he hadn't been accepted for the army or the militia on account of being short-sighted. At a certain time he would go to his canteen, because there was no way he could afford to miss his lunch there – they might not tear out the ration coupon (it did sometimes happen in that canteen). After lunch he returned to the office, where there was still plenty of work. Then he would go back home, because there was still supposed to be an evening meal, and besides there was nowhere else to go. Tanya had gone, after saying all there was to say – that she was going away and leaving him (of course he had egged her on to go) not at all because . . . on the contrary, because . . . Friends and colleagues had gone off to the front or just gone. He had his supper and turned in immediately; since he'd got up at six, he felt sleepy by ten in the evening.

But this tenor of existence, precise and unquestioned, in the main directed by the triad of eating-times, was still not a regimen, but rather the lifeless sketch of one. A regimen exists for some purpose. N was no stranger to the dystrophic idea of restoring his strength, an idea which had been motivating all sorts of things – in particular the total subordination of time to the three stages of eating. But he was asking by now: What point is there in restoring my strength? He would not have asked that if he had been fighting or standing by a lathe in a factory. But he was the periphery of a war, almost blended with the front line but divided from it by the different quality of its unfreedom. In the peripheral world, everything was for the moment negative. Even work. Even the most useful behind-the-lines work was located in the

same sphere as food, and worries about the stove and water. By the painful effort of a will used to a monotonous series of gestures, somewhere, at some point, he had to widen the sphere and insert a *deed* into it. If a person can write, shouldn't he write about this and what had preceded it? Somewhere, let's say after his domestic chores, there should be an hour or more when he could write (the rotating movement of dystrophic life would not yield more). Then all the other particles of the day would come alive and tend towards that hour of the day, shaping themselves hierarchically around it.

Perhaps in the morning during his domestic tasks like carrying out the slop bucket or cleaning out the stove, he could think things over. Or as he was on his way to the bread shop or the canteen. You couldn't think in queues and you couldn't think or write after lunch. That was the time of despondency. It got better towards evening. In the hours of searing misery after lunch one shouldn't think anyway. Better sit in the office and work (it was bad for those who didn't work and just had to sit and starve) and abstractedly hear the voices of colleagues (it was good to hear voices around!).

And was it so necessary to write? Did one really have to write any more? Or was there only one deed left – head for the front! Fight against the Germans . . . Anything else was a snare and a delusion.

But those who had seen the things that writers wanted to write about would never need for others to write for them about it, about anything at all . . . But the memory refuses to give way; it stands firm and oblivion stands firm. Forgetfulness preserves life by perpetually renewing vitality, desires and delusions. It returns to life the hustle and bustle it needs – after a mortification of the flesh and spirit so measureless that any such return seems impossible.

The elastic substance of life stretches till it can stretch no more; but now the tension lessens, is released and the elastic at once recoils backwards to resume its age-old dimensions

20

and form. That which is revealed to a man in extreme situations is closed off again. Otherwise the people of our generation, for example, would have long ago ceased to be fit to carry on living.

Not a metaphysical substance, not the self-sufficient soul of the nineteenth century, but rather an endless change of situations, evoking reactions and reflexes. Let it be so, but each time, some relatively established system of biological and social data turns up in the situation, constituting itself into a unique – and at the same time typical – aggregation (the individual character) and yet we keep on being surprised – either at the unchanging character of human beings (forgetting nothing and learning nothing) or at their fickleness. Meanwhile both principles act reciprocally. The established system is continually adapting itself to changing situations and at the same time, constantly striving to return to its original state.

Tolstoy understood the reversibility of extreme situations. He knew that the sky of Austerlitz would part asunder for only an instant; that Pierre in the interval between the barrel of the French rifle and the Tsarist prison cell would again be a liberal gentleman.

But it seemed to us then . . . Of course it did: it seemed that after this it would hardly be possible to chatter away again about, say, the lyric hero* . . . Yes, we thought . . .; but why, by whom was it established, that dystrophy was the reality

* A term formulated by the famous Formalist critic Yury Tynianov in 1921 to signify a poet's lyric "double" (cf. the German *lyrisches Ich*), or "persona" in the broadest application (a literary alter ego, whether obviously mythologized or not). At the time when Ginzburg wrote *Notes from the Blockade*, the strongly negative connotations of the Formalist approach in Soviet official culture made discussions of issues such as the "lyric hero" seem more intellectually rarified and abstract than would have been the case in the modern Anglo-American world, or for that matter would be the case in Russia today. Ginzburg wrote a highly influential work of literary scholarship *On Lyric Poetry (O lirike)*, first published in 1964.

and ordinary life a delusion? That after one glance at reality you would not want illusion?

Thus we observe the law of forgetfulness, one of the cornerstones of social existence; along with the law of remembrance – the law of history and art, guilt and remorse. Herzen said of it: "He who could live through it must have the strength to remember."

Perhaps N too would battle through to his free hour and it would seem all too short to him. He would pine for more and run mentally through all the hours of the day, to gain another half-hour somewhere, another twenty minutes. The sense of lost time, that was the start of recovery. The start of recovery was when it seemed to be too long to wait forty minutes in a queue for a cup of wishy-washy coffee with saccharine.

For the moment this was only a daydream. For the moment, the main thing was to rationalize his domestic routine. To find an automatism of movement in place of convulsive movements. Automatism was a correctly solved problem and the exactness of the solution was felt by both the muscles and the mind. More and more often nowadays he managed to catch the correct movement – lifting a bucket or sawing a plank on his own or in pairs. Sawing was a particularly infallible test of movement. Once he had found a smooth rhythm, without pressing, the teeth no longer jammed and caught individually, but suddenly blended together and it was no longer the man wielding the saw but the saw drawing the effortless hand after it. And the path of the saw, like the correct path of any mechanism was accompanied by the right noise – the steady broad swishing sound of a saw. Then a man suddenly becomes aware of his stance and feels that this is the real sawyer's stance; he has leaned forward in just the right way, thrusting one leg out, and bending the other at the knee. He has found the bodily projection of the process and so experiences satisfaction.

In the morning you have to chop small logs of firewood for the stove to last the whole day. And when the axe comes down and strikes just the right spot every time without gouging, and the log splits in two, easy and dry – that's nice. It wasn't nice chopping up furniture for the stove and seeing the familiar arms, carving and metal fitments under the axe, recognizing the shape of the leg, the doors. It was like a housewife who has had a pet hen slaughtered; she prefers to eat it as cutlets, the shape of wing, leg and claw bothers her.

After that came the urgent job of taking out the slops. N treated this matter-of-factly, as it was of vital importance. He would hunch up as if trying to establish a distance between himself and the smelly bucket. It was the day's first sally outside and it had its own delight. It was a venturing-forth from a room surrounded by the yawning of an abandoned flat, a room where there reigned isolation and a chaos not wholly subdued. A going-forth into an objectively existent world . . .

In the summer of '42, there were few people in the city and very few factories; the Leningrad air had a new cleanliness. N sees the granite curve of the embankment, the patterned grille behind which stands the stagnant, colourless water, coagulated with filth. The mental associations he feels that morning are somehow all country ones – from his being unaccustomed to summer in the city, the oddly clean air, the emptiness, the quietness and because people are coming outside almost barefoot with their buckets.

N raises his bucket over the drain and quickly, without looking, tips it all into the water. A feeling of relief . . . A feeling of relief blends with a momentary lightening of exist-ence. The breeze blew through his hair. With a physical pang he recalled a village street, apple trees behind a fence. He used to spend his summers there as a teenager; his mother used to send him to the neighbours for milk. He used to carry the milk in a jug, stepping gingerly though the dust so as not to

spill any. The point was the simultaneity of the sensations: bare feet treading the fine dust of the road and in his hands the earthenware warmed by the sun.

Anyway he had always loved beautiful natural contexts. Not the scenery you admire from a distance, rather the nature that was ever-present, always a part of any human enterprise. It was good to go down to a stream and wash; clean your teeth while up to your ankles in water, and the sunlight glancing along the water and the leaves heaving and rustling close by on the other bank.

Then, in a precisely established order, comes the trip out to the baker's or to a shop if there was anything being given out. The trams go by, people go off to work and to the shops. But, oddly enough, the city is as neat and quiet as before. The asphalt gleams warmly in the light of the sun, as yet low in the sky. It is good and right that the city should be proud of a well-swept street, while bombed-out houses stand along both sides; that is the social network of things continuing and returning.

The everyday routes go past houses which have been bombed in different ways. There are sections of houses which keep reminding you of Meyerhold's theatre sets.* There are sections of small multi-coloured rooms with the little round stove still intact, painted the same colour as the wall, or an intact door, sometimes ajar. Grim stage-set doors, carefully made and leading nowhere. The house sections illustrate the storeys, the thin layers of floor and ceiling. You begin

* Vsevolod Meyerhold (1874–1940), a towering figure in the world of Russian-Soviet theatre, began his career in acting (played in many roles at the Moscow Art Theatre) and then became a director, staging plays in both Moscow and Petersburg. He invented a system of acting called "biomechanics", and was close to the symbolists, futurists, constructivists, and other avant-garde groups. He was arrested in 1939 and executed in 1940.

to realize with astonishment that as you sit at home in your room you are suspended in space, with other people similarly suspended over your head and beneath your feet. You know about this of course, you've heard furniture being moved about upstairs, even wood being chopped. But all that is abstract, unpicturable, like the way we are borne along through space on a sphere rotating about its axis. Everybody feels as if their floor rests on some kind of soil, covered over with planking. Now the truth had been revealed in a dizzyingly graphic fashion. There were skeletal houses with preserved facades, shot through with darkness and depth. And the sky can be seen through the empty window sockets of the upper storeys. There were houses, especially small ones, whose beams and flooring had collapsed under their crumbling roofs. They hung at an angle and looked as if they were still sliding down, perpetually falling, like a waterfall.

A new attitude to houses developed.

People began to talk about houses, think about houses. The accepted unit of the city became the apartment house, just as previously it had been the street, with its merged undifferentiated facades. Unobservant people suddenly saw what constituted their city. It was made up of discrete areas of incomparable Leningrad beauty, out of astonishing complexes of stone and sky, water and foliage, and for the rest, of apartment houses of the second half of the nineteenth century, with a certain trace of pre-revolutionary modern and boxes dating from the first years of the revolution. The wretched architecture of the second half of the last century, with its fear of line and plane, the flat surface and the unfilled space, which prompted it to cram every unoccupied space with some sort of stucco nonsense. Now we saw these houses, shabby and bare, standing in damp and rusty streams of poor-quality paint. In the grim autumn days it seemed that this rusty dankness was oozing out from inside them. They presaged nothing good.

A new attitude to houses developed. Each house was now a defence and a threat. People used to count the storeys, and it was a double calculation – how many storeys would protect them and how many would fall on them. We learned about volumes, proportions, building materials. Houses began to be regarded analytically. They were divided into vaults, ceilings, stairwells. "Stairwells" had an especially grisly sound. Coming down the back stairs of their dwellings, people looked closely at sundry projections and cluttered niches, about which they had been ignorant before. Now they were refuges. Which would be better if anything happened – to lean against the right wall here or the left? Sometimes people would try and imagine the unimaginable: suppose these projections and steps, suspended aloft, actually were to collapse in an instant and fall on your head or your chest. The stairwell cage crushing the ribcage* . . . Ribcage – that too was special and grisly.

If a house is regarded analytically, then the city by contrast is apprehended synthetically. It is no longer a series of instantaneous combinations of streets, houses and buses. The city is a synthetic reality. It is the city which struggles, suffers, repulses the killers. This general concept is a material one. We perceive the city now as if from an aeroplane, as if on a map. It is an objective whole delimited by a visible border. The outposts close off the frontier; gates break up the frontier (the city has doors, like any human dwelling house). The enemy attempts to force the gates; the outposts and gates do not let him approach.

We have once more attained something unknown to modern man – the reality of city distances, long ago swallowed up

* In Russian there is a pun that is impossible to translate, but contributes to the "grisly" nature of this image: *Lestnichnaia kletka razdavila grudnuiu kletku*, meaning "the stair cage [stairwell] crushed the ribcage".

by trams, buses and taxis. A city plan has appeared, with the islands, the branching Neva, a visual system of regions, because in winter, without trams, without telephones, friends who lived on Vasilievsky, the Vyborg side or the Petrograd Side didn't meet for months on end and died unnoticed by one another.

The various regions took on new qualities. There were regions which were fired on and regions which were favourite targets for air raids. Sometimes, crossing a bridge meant entering a zone of altered possibilities. There were border regions which had prepared themselves to withstand the storm. Thus the significance of short distances increased. The city's rivers had become a military fact, the bridges across them with their anti-aircraft batteries had become a military fact. The rivers divided the regions with their special characteristics. They were a potential frontier. And you could imagine a war across these regions and between them.

From the beginning of the war, the city had begun to sprout unusual details. First of all there appeared the cross-shaped stickers on the windows (so that the glass wouldn't shatter). This measure had been suggested to the populace in the very first days of the war. In the midst of the uncertain despondency of those first days, when the shape of the new life had not yet been defined, this mechanical activity had a soothing effect, distracting people from the emptiness of merely waiting. But there was something poignant and strange about it too, reminiscent for example of a sparkling surgical ward, where there were as yet no wounded, but where there certainly would be.

Some people stuck the strips on in a rather intricate pattern. One way or another, the rows of windows with their paper stickers took on the form of ornament. From a distance on a sunny day it looked cheerful, recalling those decorative fretted scallops you see on the wooden huts of prosperous peasants. But everything changed if you looked closely at the stickers on the lowest windows in bad weather. The yellowing of

the damp paper, the blobs of paste, dirty newsprint showing through, the roughly trimmed edges – are the symbolism of death and destruction, which had not yet had time to settle and attach itself to the cross-shaped pieces of paper.

Later on, house and shop windows started being boarded up. Some people boarded up their windows because the glass had shattered, others so as to stop it doing so. Sometimes fresh, almost white sheets of plywood were involved, sometimes rough, very drab planking. Boarded-up windows marked an abandoned dwelling. But in the autumn, the houses were not yet empty; the three million encircled population still crammed them to the eaves. In those autumn days, the symbol of the boarded-up windows took on a grim reverse significance – it became a mark of people buried alive, and perishing as they were, jammed together; it had the funeral symbolism of boards, immuring people in cellars, and the weight of upper storeys collapsing on them.

The city was filled with a monotonous patchwork of details, expressive, individually various, but collated into a single whole. Windows jutted out from the dank walls, boarded up with fresh plywood, or old planks, stuck over with paper – blue wrapping-paper, coloured paper, newspapers – or just bricked up. Sometimes in one window, there were areas of plywood, brick and glass stuck over with paper. The signs were uncertain and confused; before having had a chance to take shape, the painful associations became blurred. Later on people ceased to care. The windows were sheathed in ice. People in the street took no notice of the houses now. They looked where they were walking, because the pavements were icy and they were afraid of falling, either from weakness or because it was slippery. They were especially afraid of falling over while carrying dinner pails full of soup.

By the time winter came, people no longer talked about the blackout (in '39, during the Finnish war, we talked about it a lot). There was no light now, you couldn't go out late

28

nor was there any reason to. It seemed that even at night it wasn't as dark, nor as frightening in the streets as it was at home. The trams (while they were still running), the trams with their blue lamps seemed a refuge. There was light inside; it might be blue but it was light, there were people managing to breathe a bit of warmth into it; there was the conductress grumbling in her matter-of-fact way . . . and a person could relax, once he had dived inside after waiting at a deserted stop.

Nowadays nobody gave a thought to the blackout or to lots of other things. One hundred and twenty-five grams*, water from a hole in the frozen Neva, the cold, which never let up, not during sleep, not at meal-times, not at work; the blackness setting in during the day and dispersing late in the morning; corpses in the gateways, corpses on sledges, lanky and thin – more like mummies than normal human corpses.

The sound used to come precisely at the appointed time, different at different periods during that autumn, varying within half an hour. But as often happens, it was just when people weren't thinking about it. Forgetting that they were expecting the sound, they would hurry away to boil up the kettle on the stove before the alert. The sound would suddenly burst out from the loudspeaker, filling all the rooms of the flat, inhabited or not. This was the way the bomb-shelter procedure began. There was a period when the evening sirens used to start around eight o'clock. German punctuality came into it as a deliberate element in their calculated mental assault.

The alerts were varied in duration, frequency and intensity; the procedure on the other hand was monotonous to the point of ritual. People donned galoshes and overcoats. They were annoyed at leaving their tea half-drunk and had

* 125 grams of bread per day was the allowance for office workers, as well as for dependants and children under twelve, from 20 November to 25 December 1941.

no desire to go down into a chilly cellar. They kept straining their ears – would it be a quiet alert? The anti-aircraft guns banged away louder and more often. Then the people would go down in the darkness feeling their way down the familiar staircase. Many had a place of their own in the cellar, where they met their friends, conversed, dozed, sometimes reading if they could get near the lamp; they went over to the door to smoke; every day they experienced the joyful relief of the all clear. After the all clear they debated whether it was worth going upstairs straight away or better to wait for the next raid (at different periods there were different considertions involved); they went back up and sometimes came back down again; then they went up for good, drank their cold tea and went to bed without undressing. There was something soothing by now in the ritual repetition of the procedure. The order of the elements included the nervous clicking of the loudspeaker, the search for galoshes in the dark, the drowsy dampness of the cellar, the rolled cigarette smoked by the door, the slow return home (the slower the better, in case the siren went again). A direct hit, collapsed ceilings and bloody porridge did not form part of this experience and therefore seemed unreal. The ritual began with the sound coming from the loudspeaker and ended with the return to a smouldering stove. That was why, against all logic, the feeling of tension used to subside as soon as people went out onto the staircase, heading for the shelter. It was the beginning of a procedure – the safe ending of which had been proved every day in practice. Many even thought that it was the actual descent and sitting in the cellar that guaranteed a happy outcome; it never occurred to them that this time the house might have survived just as well if they had stayed upstairs in their apartments. Such an obvious idea would have astonished them.

In the morning people would learn of the night's events. They would look at the apartment houses ripped asunder and the savagely rent existence of man, shuddering with revulsion

at the act which had taken place here. And in the evening the set procedure took over again.

Sometimes in the bomb shelter the empty quiet hours dragged on. It seemed then that for some reason this couldn't go on, it was all over. Then all of a sudden came a rounded noise accompanied by a deep shudder in the earth. It was actually a thud, rounded and welling up. But at the same time it always seemed like a noise. The people in the cellar would lift their heads and look at one another. "Somebody's caught it," a voice would say. The men would debate listlessly where it had fallen and what weight it was.

The forever unforgettable experience of time turned upside down. The ungraspably brief present, which for the sitters here became the past before fear could penetrate their minds; while elsewhere for someone it was by now replete with vast, horrific content, had already become the end of everything or the beginning of a long agony.

The exaggerated role of dinner, the ritual sitting in the cellar. The limit of unfreedom and of the denial of the value of the person. It could only be avoided at the price of direct participation in the war.

The general attitude to bombs, shelling, to deadly danger altered several times, depending on the fate of the city, the general military situation.

In besieged Leningrad we saw everything – but fear least of all. People heard the whistle of shells over their heads with indifference. Waiting for a shell you know is coming is considerably harder; but everyone knew that if you heard it, it wasn't going to land on you this time.

The quantification of degrees of jeopardy, or more precisely, the probability of death (the degree of probability) is of decisive psychological importance. Between certain death and almost certain death there is fixed an unbridgeable gulf. In Leningrad the peril was an everyday matter, systematic, and systematically designed to wear out the nerves, but

statistically it wasn't very great. Everyday experience showed that the danger from bombing and shelling paled before the enormous toll of death by dystrophy. To this slow form of death, a man passed through quite a different inner preparation. The attitude to the shell or bomb in Leningrad was of course different from at the front or the inhabitants of towns set ablaze by air raids later on.

In Leningrad there were few who were afraid of the bombing – just those with some special physiological predisposition to fear. It soon became impossible to run anywhere. Therefore nobody fled and nobody thought: Why am I staying when everybody's leaving? Composure marked the universal and average behaviour, noncompliance with which was harder and more terrible than the actual dangers. In order to keep a cool head amid a general panic, you have practically got to be a hero. But try shouting and running about when all around you are doing their bit – you have to be bold indeed to do that.

On one occasion, I happened to be caught during an air raid in a hairdresser's, when they were still working normally, and I observed how the ordinary girls carried on with their six-monthly perms to the sound of anti-aircraft fire, exchanging remarks about how terrible it was.

Death can be successfully suppressed for the very reason that it is not accessible to experience. It's an abstraction of non-existence or the emotion of fear. In the first case it belongs to the category of unimaginable imaginings (like eternity, endlessness). In order to conceive of an instant transition from a room and a person to a chaos of brick, metal and flesh, and above all, nonexistence – this is a work of imagination beyond the capacity of many.

The artist X (a good artist) differed from the majority of Leningraders in his fear of the bombing. He moved in with friends because they lived on lower floors. Their daughter, about twelve, would look in on him while he was restlessly

32

pacing about the room: "Come and have some tea. They'll soon be finished." (They – were the Germans). He would reply: "You have no imagination, that's why you're not afraid. You have to be really clever, you know, to be afraid properly."

To the extent that fear of death is an emotion, it is subject to all the whims and inconsistencies of emotions. It crops up and subsides quite without reference to the laws of reason which register an objective danger, but rather according to the play of impulses and reflexes. Here I am recalling things said long ago. For example, it is possible to wake up in bed at the most peaceful of times, numb with terror at the thought of inevitable extinction – and one can wander about under fire abstracted and indifferent (in the one case you're concentrating at night with nothing to distract you, in the other your attention is diverted). The nerves of a man afflicted with a philosophical dread of death may be well-adjusted to specific shocks and whistles – or it may be the other way about.

Not to think about mortal danger, when actually heading for it, is sometimes easier than to go to work without thinking about the official reprimand you have received. There is no other area where the power of social pressure is so glaringly obvious.

From very ancient times and up to today the word coward has been a magic word. You can be afraid of catching cold, but being afraid of death is shameful. How could this have been instilled into humanity, with its will for self-preservation, how was it inculcated? It was probably successful because otherwise the existence of society or state would be altogether impossible and because all available means of pressure had been deployed in this area.

This is the story told by M, a middle-aged woman; at the beginning of the war, she worked in some organization in Leningrad as a typist. Gradually everybody left the city. Her organization, like a number of others, was still formally functioning. When the war started, night duties were introduced

33

for the staff in the director's office just in case. On the eighth of September M was on duty. Every day at around 20.00 hours the Germans would make their pedantic presence felt with a false alarm. This had become a routine part of the day. M took a book with her so that afterwards she could lie down on the sofa and doze till morning. At 20.00 came the alert. Just as usual; it would be over and she could have a lie down. But suddenly there came something new, unprecedented. Not quite a noise, not quite a jolt – for the noise and jolt were one and the same. The floor shuddered heavily, the lamp began shaking on the ceiling. Again it happened, and again. If it hadn't been for the blacked-out windows, the glow from the Badaevsky warehouses would have been visible, burning with Leningrad's grain inside them. The first bombs of this first raid had fallen close to the office. The office was purely civilian and no use to anyone in those days. But the duty officer had to be on duty by the director's telephone in case of – what? Orders most likely. M was standing in the middle of the office; the air-raid shelter was three floors below. The floor shook again. Meanwhile the director's telephone on the bronze-fitted desk stood mute. To leave it was cowardly, uncitizenlike. Thoughts of cowardice, the fear of revealing cowardice and the simultaneous thought of the pointlessness of hazarding herself so completely occupied her mind that she had no time to feel genuine physical terror. She went out onto the landing and came back, went out again and returned, feeling that mortal terror and self-preservation were being firmly suppressed by a kind of numbness. In the director's office the radio ticked away nervously. To keep loneliness or some new access of anguish at bay, M aimlessly picked up the telephone. No connection followed. Absolute silence – so the line must be damaged somewhere. Then she went downstairs. Several people crowded round the entrance to the shelter. One had a hastily bandaged head. They had run in from the next street, from the first house to be hit.

A colleague, the head of the local PVO* was nosing about the corridor. He was prepared for anything, death included. "Why on earth are you not at your posts? Everybody on duty! What are you doing here?" "The telephone line's cut . . ." But he wasn't listening to her; he went on shouting as he ran along the corridor. He had no right at all to give her orders and nobody was stopping her going down to the cellar. But she didn't do it. The house trembled and shook yet again. She slowly made her way upstairs to the director's office and laid her hand on the lifeless telephone. As she did so she recalled that it was not permitted to ring home (in September private telephones were still working) and that perhaps her husband already knew that bombs had fallen in that area. It had gone quiet. The dimmed light was flickering for some reason. She slowly went down the staircase. Not to the shelter – just to stand in the lower corridor.

She had had no time to experience real fear on that occasion. Real fear excludes everything else as if it didn't exist. She had been too preoccupied with other things – thoughts of how to conceal her fear and do what everyone else was doing or how senseless was all that she and everyone else was doing in that by now pointless organization.

She went back home early next morning; there was a dense knot of people in a nearby street. Intent and silent, they were studying a crater in the asphalt, their first crater.

People from the outside world finding themselves in Leningrad were at a loss. They would ask: "Why are none of you afraid? How do you do it?" The reply would come: "Living here for 18 months, starving, freezing . . . Well, it just can't be explained."

It's not enough to put it down just to habit. Habit only weakens the impulses of fear and self-preservation, helps to

* *Protivovzdushnaya oborona*: air-raid warden.

suppress them, replace them with other things. What you had to do was acquire other impulses, all-absorbing, all-suppressing in their pristine power.

The blockade person of autumn '41 was replaced by the blockade person of winter '41–'42. Here is this person walking along the street during shelling. He knows it is very dangerous and frightening. But he's going to the canteen for his lunch. And instead of being frightened, he's annoyed (they won't even let you have your lunch in peace . . .); instead of being afraid of death, he's afraid of being stopped on the way and herded into shelter, to prevent him hazarding his life. The possibility of being killed is present in this man's mind, but his immediate sensation is hunger, more precisely the fear of hunger, and his hungry urgency, blindly intent on its goal. One can be conscious of a number of things at the same time, but one can't desire them all at the same time with equal intensity.

A person is woken up at night by the air-raid siren. The hope of a *quiet* alert is of short duration. The sound of the anti-aircraft guns gets nearer. What a sharp crack that was! Or is it a bomb already? He is no longer thinking of getting up, looking for his galoshes and heading for the freezing cellar. He's thinking that he ought not to go to sleep again. He doesn't want *that* to happen while he's asleep. He doesn't want to wake up to find the world falling about his ears, meeting his death in the tiniest fleeting moment. Better to be prepared. Better to lie awake, listening to the approaching thuds. Better a slow introduction to catastrophe. He thinks he ought not to go to sleep, but in a few minutes, he drops off because he's tired.

What was going on was terrifying in the extreme. Right at this moment, at any instant, before he could pull up the blanket, before he could let out the breath which was now inflating his chest, this reality now present to his senses could be replaced by another – incredible, howling, jangling, from an extremity of suffering toppling into non-existence.

36

All this is so, but he hasn't the strength to be afraid. He wants to go to sleep. He's astonished at the person he was formerly. That person used to wake up at one or two in the morning at the sound of the alert. That sound was enough for him to leave his warmed-up bed instantly for the freezing cellar. That was the naïve purity and freshness of the instinct of self-preservation, as yet uneroded by exhaustion and the unceasing struggle against suffering. The upshot of this struggle – the bed warmed by the body, the body peacefully lying in the bed – had become a good, a desire, which could no longer be overmastered by the intellectual stuff of fearful imaginings.

I know it's terrifying. I want to live. If it happens, my last conscious moment will be a curse on my lack of prudence. I know I ought to be afraid and take precautions. But I'm not afraid and I can't be afraid because I want to go to sleep.

The blockade person of the summer of '42 . . . Novel nuances have appeared in his reactions. By now, it's just a routine nervous tension; it vanishes along with the irritant. The moment of the all clear is a physical pleasure of a kind, an easing, like when a toothache suddenly stops. Hence these apparently odd changes of key, odd in their rapidity. Here they are, having just had their ears pricked for death, and now it's already chatter, office gossip, women livening up over how to get hold of stockings or alter dresses.

Neither staunch feelings nor imagination play any part in nervous reaction, the conscious will can't withstand it. The mighty impulses of resilience contrive to transmute all that. Those in whom these impulses do not work were in the position of invalids.

Why was hunger, as the Germans realized, the most powerful underminer of resistance? Because hunger is a permanent state, it can't be switched off. It was constantly present and always made its presence felt (not invariably in a desire to eat); the most desperate and tormenting thing of all during the process

of eating was when the food drew to an end with awful rapidity without bringing satiety.

The purpose of venturing outside in the morning is – the shop. The grocery shop substitutes for the bakery as well. There is even a sign on the door: BREAD SOLD HERE. Is that not a pressing invitation to customers? It is rather empty and quiet in the shop now. The salesgirls are wearing their white uniforms and dummy goods shine on the shelves, irritating the customers, the registered ones that is, while the counter is laden with items which are not yet on issue and are not for sale.

Nowadays, this is rather reminiscent of the pitiless cleanliness of an out-patient clinic; in taking care of you they make you feel angry and fearful by the implacability of their procedures. Chilled by the white corridors, the white gowns, the smell that makes your heart sink, the terrifying metallic implements under the glass – by now you are not hating your illness but whatever it is that wants to save you from it.

The shop, with its unshakeable laws (they won't accept a torn-out ration coupon or issue bread for the day after tomorrow) is a fairly well-organized system of undernourishment. Loaves are neatly packed along the shelves of the bread department. There are so many of them and they smell so warm, the girl takes them so lazily from the shelf – there are no outward signs of their being forbidden fruit. The bread lies there, it costs one rouble twenty-five or one rouble ten a kilo, you get your ration without having to queue, no bother at all . . . But it's taboo. It's almost irrational.

During the winter, on the other hand, everything had been logical. There were vast impassable crowds in the shop, a hubbub of voices, threatening and imploring. The assistants struggled with the crowd across the counter. In the winter there were days when the pipes in the city froze up completely and people got water through holes in the river ice. The bakeries began to issue less than the ration. From four or

five in the morning, hundreds of people queued for bread in the freezing darkness. A person suddenly remembers how he stood in line for the first time. He stood there thinking that he wouldn't get what he wanted in any case; it was impossible, incredible (he hadn't eaten anything since the soup of the day before). But all at once he thought that even if this lasted another five hours, or six, or seven – time would still be passing and would certainly pass over these five or six hours – however full those hours might be with agonies of immobility for the individual person – therefore time itself would bear him on towards his goal. The bread shop was on the corner, and before it a boarded-up shop with a long sign: MEAT, VEGETABLES, GAME. In an hour and a half he had got past the word MEAT, then he passed VEGET and got stuck on the A for a long time. In the queue the vast idea of a piece of bread was taking shape, whereas the sign embodied the infernal torpor of the queue.

Nowadays everything was astonishingly easy (it was like the astonishment of a man who braces himself to lift a heavy suitcase and finds it to be empty). You could reach out and touch the bread across the counter. The only thing stopping you was the common convention, the abstract social taboo.

There might be a bread shortage during the winter (after which it returned to normal), queues made sense. But there were other queues which were the result of starvation mania. On the day announced for the issue of fats and "confectionery" there was a crowd outside the shop by five in the morning. People withstood all the agonies of an hours-long queue, knowing that by ten or eleven in the morning the shop would be empty. From the moment they became a possibility, it was psychologically impossible to sleep or busy yourself with anything else, or simply exist, without joining in the process of approaching the fats and confectionery.

A queue is an assembly of people, doomed to a compulsory idle and internally isolated communality. Idleness, unless it be given point by way of recreation or diversion, is just suffering,

a punishment (prison, queue, waiting to be received). A queue is complete idleness coupled with a grievous expenditure of physical energy. Men cope particularly badly with queues, since they are used to the idea that their time is valuable. The point is not even in the objective situation, it's simply a matter of inherited habits. Working women have inherited from their grandmothers and mothers time which is not taken into account. Their everyday lives do not allow that atavism to lapse. A man considers that after work he is entitled to rest or amuse himself; when a working woman comes home, she works at home. The siege queues were inscribed into an age-old background of things being issued or available, into the normal female irritation and the normal female patience.

On the other hand, almost every one of the men who turned up in a shop tried to get to the counter before his turn. Men can't explain whence comes this feeling of inner rightness despite the outward unfairness of their action. But one thing they do know – a queue is women's business. Perhaps they have a vague inkling that the justice of their claims rests on the fact that there are so few of them in the queue. They don't argue their case, however, they're either rude or they come out with the classic phrase: "I'm in a hurry to get to work." "And we aren't?! (It's always *we*; a man in a queue feels like a stray individual, a woman is the representative of a collective). Everybody's in a hurry to get to work nowadays," flares a woman with a briefcase. The man stealthily conceals his bread when he gets it. He has nothing to say; but inwardly he knows that even if she works as much as he does, or even more, their attitude to time, its value, use and allocation are different. And that attitude gives him the right to get bread without queuing for it. The shop girl, not being involved, understands this – usually she encourages the claims of the men.

Very few people read a book in a queue, or even a newspaper. That will surprise only those who have never stood for hours

40

every day in queues. The psychology of the queue is based on a tense, wearing anxiety to reach the end, an inward urging-forward of empty time; this weariness excludes anything else that might relieve it. The mental state of a person standing in a long queue is usually not fitted for any other occupation. The intellectual may naïvely take a book along, but he prefers to keep track of what's going on. Having elbowed his way sideways to the counter, he watches the girl giving out the bread to those in front. With an inward forward-thrusting shudder, he reacts to any slowing down of her gestures (if she leaves the counter for an instant, it's agony, like when a train stops suddenly), or he joins pleasurably in the deft rhythm of her work, or rejoices at any chance gain in time (for example, if someone has his ration book thrust back at him – he's not registered with that shop).

A person will go into genuine hysterics over one queue-jumper who edges in front of him – and then after getting his ration, the same person will stand for half an hour chatting to a friend, talking freely now, like someone here of his own free will. While he was in the queue, he was caught up, like all the rest, in the physical craving for movement, however illusory. Those at the back shout to those in front: "Come on, get a move on, what's the hold up?" And there'd be some philosopher, ignorant of the mechanics of mental states, who will be sure to respond: "Why push up? It'll be no quicker for that."

The dystrophic winter queues were eerily silent. Gradually, with the increase in the bread ration, the spring warmth and the appearance of greens in the shops (people used to buy and boil vegetable leaves), the mores of the queue underwent a change. It began to converse. Human beings abhor a vacuum. The immediate filling-up of a vacuum is one of the basic functions of the word. Pointless conversations in our lives are no less important than meaningful ones.

The course of a conversation is, in its way, determined, but the springs are hidden from the talkers. Subjectively they

41

are carrying out an act almost independent of opposition from an objective world, which hangs heavy over every deed. Conversation is a free surrogate of a law-governed activity. It is a vague prototype of art, also a special sort of reality, where a person himself creates and destroys the objects which inhabit it.

Conversation is a model of the passions and emotions; love and vanity, hope and anger find in it a transparent embodiment. Conversation is wish-fulfilment. In conversation over a cup of tea or a glass of wine, inaccessible barriers are scaled, ends are achieved, which in the world of deeds would take years of failure and effort.

Conversation is a process of discharging; it is the objectivization of desires, values, ideals, abilities and possibilities – cognitive, aesthetic, volitional. Above all, a conversation with one's fellow human being is a most powerful medium of self-assertion, a declaration of one's personal value. Utterance achieves realization and a social existence – this is one of the basic laws of behaviour.

In his dialogue with another, a person asserts himself both directly and obliquely, head on and in roundabout fashion – from plain boastfulness and naïve talk about himself and his affairs to secret admiration of his own opinions about science, art, politics, his own wit and eloquence, his hold over the attention of his listener. Self-assertion has concealed itself in the objectively interesting, has taken the form of information or the aesthetically meaningful. Sometimes the information is only a pretext, sometimes the assertion of self merely accompanies the information. One way or another, self-assertion is the imperishable psychological essence of conversation.

There are extreme situations – the existentialists call then limit situations – when it seems that everything must change. In actual fact the perpetual motion machines carry on their great work (Tolstoy discovered that). It is just that what was concealed becomes obvious, the approximate – literal;

everything becomes condensed, manifest. This is what the conversation of blockade person in queues, air-raid shelters, in canteens, in editorial offices, eventually became.

A queue is a compulsory agglomeration of people, irritated with one another, yet at the same time concentrating on a single common circle of interests and aims. Hence the mixture of rivalry, hostility and collective feeling, the instant readiness to close ranks against the common enemy – the law-breaker. The conversations here are loosened by the enforced idleness and at the same time held together by the fixed nature of the content, concerned as it is with the business of the queue.

The matter of obtaining food naturally requires utterances of a communicative nature (Who's last in the queue? Which coupon? Up to what coupon? Have they got "Southern" sweets today? Is it true the "Iran" sweets are paper-wrapped – not worth it then!) – as well as those employed in the fight against the law-breaker. Formally speaking, they are also communicative in nature (aimed at achieving a practical result). In actual fact, however, the practical element in them is paltry, just as the value of time is for a housewife, when she spends it on some queue intruder. Nor is the sense of legality she appeals to of any major significance in her everyday mental make-up. The practical effect of remarks like these is to conceal the discharge of irritation, impatience, all the accumulated emotions. Their emotional essence is confirmed by the motiveless asperity and venom that accompanies the answer to harmless questions: "Do you happen to know what coupon it is, on the worker's ration?" or: "And how do you cook them?" "What, is this the first time you've ever got rations?" "What, you've never cooked them?" (Here the suspicion emerges that you are dealing with a lady who thinks she's above such things.) During the winter there was no asking anybody about anything, the least enquiry was a longed-for excuse for a savage reply which relieved anger and torment. In better times, along with rude answers, one

might come across a voluble and circumstantial reply – the responder enjoying his role as guide and adviser.

But the soul of the queue is in the other conversation, the one filling up the vacuum of idleness, severely determinate and illusorily free. Conversation about food – a matter of life and death – within the unpretentious envelope of a house-wife's professional interests.

For intellectuals, for young people, even for men in general, this conversation has novelty, the ban has just been removed from it; they create in it various kinds of awkward, new and expressive turns of phrase. They can't resist it, but they're ashamed of it as a mark of degradation. For the housewife it is a continuation of her age-old conversation. For the house-wife of the pre-war period, there is nothing new in either queues or coupons, or the question "What are they giving out?" So there was no need to refurbish the phraseology in any radical fashion.

All the same, something had altered. In the first place this conversation had squeezed out all her other professional conversations (about school, shopping, cleaning-women). Secondly, this conversation, which had previously drawn down the scorn of men and businesswomen (especially young ones) and which she had been forbidden to inflict upon the thinking man – this conversation had triumphed. It had taken on a universal social meaning and importance, paid for by the terrible experience of the winter. A conversation on how it's better not to salt millet when boiling, because then it gets to be just right, had become a conversation about life and death (the millet expands, you see). Reduced in range (siege cuisine), the conversation became enriched with tales of life's ups and downs, difficulties overcome and problems resolved. And as the basic element of the given life situation, it subsumed every possible interest and passion.

When this queue conducts a conversation about food, every-thing is included in it: emotional discharge in the reproaches

44

and complaints, informative generalization in discussions on the best ways of obtaining, cooking and sharing food, the retailing of "interesting stories" – and self-assertion of every kind. Another feature is the declaration of your superiority over others, still in this same area of getting, cooking and allocating food and on the same lines, some story about yourself, your own personality, with everything that relates to it or has to do with it – psychological observations, factual details up to and including the simplest statement: "In our canteen we've had some cabbage soup off the ration, it's very thin though . . ."

"What if they are sprats? I put them through the mincer with a pat of butter. When my husband comes home he has a bit. It's nice anyway."

The blunt assertion of one's achievements. But *pat* of butter, *he'll have a bit* – are endearing forms applied to vitally important things.

"And how do you boil it?"

"I cook it like cabbage soup. Like any greens. You'd think you didn't know . . ."

This sharpness is just in case, prophylactic. What if the question had been put by someone with lily-white hands, thinking she was above it all . . . and thus superior to the one answering the question.

"I personally got a new lease of life as soon as the greens appeared."

"Right from the start we boiled nettles and goosefoot as well."

"No, I used raw nettles exclusively. Quite a different sensation."

The old-fashioned intellectual turns of phrase (I personally, exclusively, sensation) overlie a theme which is common to everybody in the queue. For intellectuals the ban has been lifted from direct conversations about oneself and food. All the same, the topic is slightly camouflaged by the common interest in self-observation or instructing one's listener.

"We've registered there again. And you should see how much they give out. My sister brought home two portions of soup, and there was literally half a tin of rice in this soup."

Facts of common significance, but in terms of the personal undercurrent – a demonstration of achievement.

"Oh no, I've started on the bread. Now I'm afraid I'll never get it home."

"You should never start on it."

A third woman (standing behind the confectionary items): "You feel better when it's finished. While it's there it draws you like a magnet. Like a magnet."

"You can't rest till you've eaten it. You can't put it out of your mind."

"Like a magnet, it draws you."

"You know, I've bought 100 grams of sweets."

"And half a kilo of bread with butter – doesn't last a minute. I'm really scared to carry it home."

The satisfaction of talking about oneself is doubled by the satisfaction gained from the exercise of the intellectual faculties. Self-observation, proceeding to the generalization of experience. "You should never start on it" is already a maxim; "like a magnet, it draws you" is a literary image.

"There you are, the child and I will eat it."

"In one day?"

"A day? In one second. Before, we used to use 200 grams of butter a day."

"Yes, for the three of us as well."

"Mine used to be hopeless. All of a sudden they don't want buckwheat porridge. Boil up oats for them. And oatmeal soup, and porridge. I say to them: one or the other – either oatmeal soup, or porridge . . . No, make both for them. Right, I boil the oats . . ."

"Well my lad – he's seven, but they know all about food nowadays. Whenever they announce a childrens' ration on the radio, he's all ears. You get sugar for children up to twelve . . .

46

He says: 'Mama, that's my sugar, I'm not giving you any.'
And I say to him: 'And I won't give you any sweets.'

This is a story about oneself, one's family; particularly about how the family used to eat – hence the universal objective interest. This is confirmed by the interrogative response of the listener ("In one day?"). In a story of how people used to eat before, there is a subtext of self-assertion: to what extent I and mine were and can rise above the things which govern us now. The answering reaction shows understanding; it indicates that the listener is also above them and belongs to the same circle, that circle of people who used to get 200 grams of butter a day for three.

The family lived so well, that the children, out of sheer perversity (from having too much, the reason gentlemen in days of yore used to eat rye bread) demanded not the best but that which was a good deal worse – thus ran the undercurrent of the story about the buckwheat and the oatmeal.

On went the eternal female conversation about children, this time on a new and fearful basis. The story of the boy, who already knew everything "about food", possesses an interest which is partly literary; but the main point is the implication that this is a boy wise beyond his years who will always fall on his feet, and who is already acting like an adult, though with a winning childish naïveté. But this life-adapted child at once comes a cropper. Because the auditor at once speaks of another boy, who also acted like a grown-up: "No, but my boy, the one who died, he shared everything. It was amazing. His father and I couldn't wait to eat. But he would hide sweets in his pocket. He would pat his pocket and say: "You're not allowed to have any more." And he was so generous. He used to give his away. He said: "Mama, you're hungry, aren't you, take some of my bread.'"

During the winter, those approaching the counter were gripped by one all-consuming passion. They hardly uttered

a word: with maniacal impatience they stared ahead over the next man's shoulder at the bread. Nowadays things are different, but even now casual conversation ceases in front of the scales. Necks crane. Facial muscles stiffen. The customer establishes contact with the seller. Both engage in a tense, silent struggle for a gram over or under. The person at the counter watches the assistant unhurriedly taking a loaf from the shelf, cutting through the crust, revealing the beautiful soft chocolate-coloured interior. She slices off, or adds solid square pieces from those lying on a board nearby; you can't take one and eat it. It's taboo. The entire vast social mechanism guards these morsels from the outstretched human hand. Nothing more lies between them – no lock, no police, no queue. Just the immense abstraction of social prohibition.

The customer's attention is riveted to the automatic scales and its moving pointer. This is partly for fear of being cheated, but mainly because he is experiencing the illusion of taking part in the vitally important weighing process. It is something like the races, where everybody races along with the horse he has backed – although he doesn't move and is powerless to affect the result of the contest. The pointer makes an initial massive swing, which gradually lessens as it fluctuates for a long time against the white disc, seeking its place among the figures. Now it has gone past the right figure – that's always unpleasant: it means that the assistant with an inexorable gesture is going to slice a square off the piece lying on the scales. It's good when the pointer doesn't reach, which means there's more to come. It means there'll be another piece, maybe quite a big one . . . no, it's really small; strange that a little bit like that can affect the pointer. This mental participation in the bread-weighing process is accompanied by a kind of absurd, doomed hope that today for some reason, the piece will be larger than ever before. If the assistant guesses the weight correctly straight away, it's hopeless. If she's a lot on the low side, that's bad too, because you're not allowed

to touch a large make-weight piece till you get home – that's siege ethics. Best of all is when there are some small make-weight pieces which don't really count and under the normal rules belong to the person getting the bread (even if there's a family at home). You're in luck if there are two really small bits. You're allowed to eat the make-weights but breaking a piece off the main ration is extremely dangerous; that way you might eat it bit by bit, before you get home to breakfast. Instead of breakfast, there will be nothing but dreary starvation at home. It's better to slice the bread with a knife. This preserves the pristine shape of the ration untouched, the straight surface of the cut – its protective covering.

During the winter, the trams went out of service gradually. In the city they would say: "The current's off today; I trudged all the way from the Petrograd side." Next day there would be some sort of service. Nobody thought it was the end. Once they failed to run for several days together, and then one overtook N on the road and picked him up. Then it all came to an end and as time went by it became a matter of cobbled roads sheathed in an icy carapace, beneath which tramlines were unimagineable, and trolley buses frozen to the roadway. They stood by the curb, trolley arms lowered.

The business of running round in circles assumed the most concrete reality – from home to the office, from office to canteen, from canteen to canteen, from the second canteen to the office . . .

In April, the city disinterred its tramlines. N and his office also participated. It took a long time for N to get used to the trams. He kept thinking that it was something in the nature of a publicity exercise and not for any practical purpose. He watched in astonishment as businesslike people crowded round the door in all seriousness shouting: "Where do you think you're pushing?" – just as if there had been no break in the service. He continued to go on foot, in order to

49

avoid the crush and the long wait, so he said; it was easier to walk. In actual fact, his ossified way of existence simply rejected the new factor. During the tram stoppage, it had contrived to harden into a series of repetitive reflex gestures.

At length he tried it – and it turned out that the trams were a practical proposition after all. At once he became an extreme devotee of tramway travel. His rationalizing reflection was that this was because it involved the least expenditure of physical effort. If truth be told, there was another more important factor – it was too grim to contemplate the space separating him from his destination, a space he would have to cover step by step with his own body, in an agony of haste. It was easier to wait. It was always a long wait.

He used to walk from the stop to the corner, from where he could see the bend. He would peer short-sightedly, suddenly mistaking the gates of a house across the way, or the foliage of a tree or a row of windows in a wall for an approaching tram. A little nearer, another tramline cut across the road. This was deceiving; still it was good that even alien trams were running and clanging – it meant that the trams were on that day. It was hard to make out which tram it was, when its dark red bulk really did appear – maybe it was a crossing tram again. But now it was clearly turning its nose his way and hauling its chassis round the curve.

The tram journey was one of the best, most uplifting moments of the day. This was humanity outwitting hostile chaos. Amid all the recalcitrant things that go slipping out of our control, all the things that have to be moved and lifted using our own muscles or willpower – all of a sudden one obedient thing, mechanical power at your service.

N takes daily pleasure in renewing an automatism of movement, almost forgotten, as he grips the stanchion, and lightly leaning back, hoists himself onto the platform. He stays on the platform. He has no rational desire now to economize on physical effort (to do that, he would have to sit down).

50

He wants to feel that wonderful mechanical movement being carried out by him and for him. The hostile world is deceived for an instant; a piece has been torn out of it.

Next to him on the platform stand two very young, handsome Red Navy men in sailor hats. To N the shuddering platform now seems like deck; on it, someone stands with legs astride, hands thrust in pockets and a papirosa* clamped between his teeth. The salt wind blows in his face. The tram moves onward, shaking and clanging at the stops. Without the aid of the passengers it pushes the street further and further away. The lower edge of the window frame slices easily through the houses, bombed or unscathed, signs no longer valid, policemen on point duty. For an instant it holds some pedestrians in shot then abandons them on the road.

Movement – clanging, rattling movement, which soothes one's haste.

Then all of a sudden, an alert. Artillery bombardment. Have to get off the tram. N goes into an entrance to a block of flats. He has been in this block quite often, seeing friends. They have left the city as well. A few steps lead up to a landing with large windows. That's bad, but on the other hand, there's a ledge to sit on.

There were people already gathered in the entrance.

"This is the start," says somebody.

The block duty woman appears: "Move away from the windows please. Come through here."

"How is this better? There's windows here as well."

A shell bursts close by.

"Come downstairs, comrades."

"Now, where are you standing, young lady? Right under the window. No need to put on a show."

People keep coming in from the street. There are quite a lot on the stairs by now.

* A short, cheap cigarette with a tubular cardboard holder.

Swearing at the Fritzes. A woman on the window-ledge is engrossed in telling another, very loudly, how she feeds herself. She doesn't eat in a canteen, because they cheat you there, and you can make things much nicer than that at home. Then come details of how she makes delicious things even nowadays, to the admiration of all.

Two men, both quite young, are discussing the destructive effect of shell splinters and whether they can penetrate one main wall or two. The male tendency to generalization, especially of a technical nature. One of them, the less intelligent of the two, is telling some confused story about a block destroyed by two shells six months before. He wants to talk about it because he was there himself and on the point of going into a bread shop in that block and it was only by happy chance that he went elsewhere. He still feels the urge to talk about it, but now he disguises the narrative in the form of an objectively relevant discussion on the penetrative power of a shell.

One girl says to another: "If they'd let me I'd go. It's just hanging about otherwise."

"You're allowed."

"No, no, we wouldn't get far."

"There's police everywhere round here. Don't go. After what happened here yesterday . . ."

"No, better if we go to your place, we could sit in the cellar."

"What cellar?"

"Yours."

"It's not mine. And I haven't got the key."

"Hasn't your auntie got it?"

"I haven't."

"I'm dog tired. I didn't sleep a wink last night. And up again at six for work. Oh, I can't stand up any longer. Let's go on the staircase and have a sit down. Have you got a newspaper?"

"What for?"

"To spread out, sit down."

"What do you need that for, just sit down."

"Have you had your meeting yet?"

"Not yet. Oh, I sometimes think, you know: what we should do now – get the trams going. Get them repaired. And let the rest . . ."

"You can't get the trams going on your own, and nothing else either. If the people aren't organized and on their toes. If you don't talk to people."

"Yes, that's true . . ."

"Well, how did you get fixed up?"

"Oh forget them. I don't want to be with them. I asked Ignatev's permission to transfer but he just gave me one of his sarcastic smiles: you don't like it here? I could offer you a separate kitchen if you like."

"Maybe that would be for the best."

"What do you mean? It's damp, dark and there's rats. A kitchen's a kitchen."

The conversation of weary people at the end of their tether. They talk about it but they carry on working. Above all, they know they have to work. And these two girls know that they have to keep people on their toes. It's a tacit agreement.

In the apartment to the left, where N had been on occasion, a dressmaker lived in a small room. She hadn't left the city. She emerges onto the staircase, seeing a client out. The customer clearly had a first-category ration card. She had that look (an actress perhaps?), here she was placing her order . . .

CUSTOMER: "What's going on outside? What's the radio say?"

DRESSMAKER: "Nothing. There'll be some singing soon."

CUSTOMER: "It's our guns firing now. Don't worry. Guns and singing songs. Makes you laugh."

"Such is life. We live and we die – death comes to us all slowly but surely. Of course, on other fronts it's all right.

Round Kharkov. But we're getting it the worst and you can't see any end to it . . ."

"It's awful! And the worst of it is that people have changed. They've got dull and hardened to it. Like a stagnant pond."

"Well, you're lively enough . . ."

"Lively! How am I lively? I'm incapable of reacting to anything. Two years ago, September the tenth, I well remember that day, the first bombs fell in our street. Two blocks away. I thought I'd go mad. When I went outside in the morning and looked at those walls, the rubble and that shattered block, I wept from sheer misery – that's when I was lively. I left the house and didn't come back for three days. I slept on the desk at work. I thought if I went back and saw that block again, I'd go mad. And what happened later on? . . . Later on I went stepping across corpses in the street. That's what. And I found it funny that they were so muffled up. And their heads lolling about. A cross between a doll and a human being. I was always frightened of surviving someone of my close family, I kept thinking about how it would be. Then I buried my grandmother and didn't feel a thing. And I used to call her mama. Well of course I cried a bit, I'm not saying I didn't."

"Your grandmother was such a wonderful old woman. Always neat and clean. I often used to meet her in the alley."

"A marvellous granny. So funny. At one time she couldn't imagine how it was possible to get married without a fox fur coat."

"Of course, they used to sew a trousseau in her day."

"She had a rotonda. I remember."

A girl standing nearby: "What's that, a rotonda?"

"They were sleeveless. You used to throw them on like a cloak. Why should a lady need sleeves? Or hands? To carry baskets with? She only used to go out to show herself off. She'd wrap herself up in this velvety rotonda – very light, it was, fox fur. And away she ran. I was very fond of my

54

grandmother. Then she died and – nothing. No, I've just grown numb, numb. Not a person at all, just dirty water. A swamp. I don't care about anything. I just don't care."

GIRL: "We don't care because we know we could die at any minute. That's why we don't care."

DRESSMAKER: "Well, you know, people can't keep reacting to things for two years on end. When you're in the front line, you can't react properly to death if your pal gets killed."

CUSTOMER: "Don't you believe it. It really does affect them up there; much more than us. After all I've been in the forward areas and I know. We were sitting in a tent up there, and when the shelling started things were blowing up everywhere. Our head of rations – young chap – was scared stiff and ran off to hide in a haystack."

"And what did you do?"

"I stayed where I was. I sat there all night. I told them I was a dystrophic, what was it to me? I had a whole tent full of tinned stuff, bread and sugar. And the orderly, Kolya, was with me. He used to ask all the time: 'Shall I pour you some more, young lady? Something to eat?' There was a captain there as well. Middle-aged. He was a fine chap – not afraid of anything. He used to go out and issue instructions. Then he'd come back, have a lie-down and a drop of vodka. In the morning we had a good laugh at our ration man. No, don't you believe it, it really does affect them. Well, I'm off."

"You're not frightened?"

"What's there to be frightened of? I'll just get a tram and be on my way."

"You're not afraid there might not be a tram?"

"Oh, I'm not afraid of anything. I'd like to find something to be afraid of."

The dressmaker wrings her hands, while the customer is busy constructing her own image, and both talk longingly of rotondas and ladies who had no use for hands. And yet they

were not in conflict with what was going on around them. They might personally complain and shy away from it all, but their criteria and values were historically correct. They know it has to be this way, because any other way is impossible. Their criterion: Hitler is a villain, the Germans are the enemy and have to be annihilated. The captain was a fine fellow, because he wasn't afraid. And I'm fine too (setting aside any motives to do with dystrophy), because I wasn't frightened and stayed in the tent, if only to finish up the tinned stuff – that's not the point. Whereas the ration chief who ran away and hid, is trash.

And so, in these confused women, and their longing for an easy life, the general will is reflected, as in a distorting mirror. This woman, too, consoling herself with the role of a dystrophic hysteric, is unconsciously doing her bit – coming here to order as nice a dress as possible, then going out immediately to the tram stop under fire.

And all the people crowded in here – the grumbling, the terrified, the alienated – obedient to the behavioural norm, are carrying out their historical function as *Leningraders*.

A middle-aged lady runs in, panting, with her young daughter and little granddaughter.

"I don't know, it's a disgrace! All the front doors are locked. We've run all the way from the bridge and all the front doors are locked. Can you believe it? It's a disgrace!"

Another woman: "What are you getting so worked up about. You're a Leningradka, aren't you? Leningraders are supposed to keep calm."

"Yes, calm. You have your health, maybe. I'm a sick woman, that's the difference. Are you an invalid?"

"Practically . . ."

"You're a second category invalid? Are you registered? No. That's the difference. Perhaps you haven't been bombed out, well I have. That's another difference . . . Damned Germans! Swine! Just lobbing shell after shell. It's high time they were damn well wiped out! What are they up to!"

Third woman: "They're annoyed. Angry because they're having a bad time. They're angry at Leningrad, because they can't get anywhere. That's why they're venting their spite on us."

"Damned swine! They can see us on their photographs, our faces are geting fatter – and it makes them mad. They'll get nothing here."

"That goes without saying. They're pretty well dug in here though."

"Yes, they've got their heads down. It's a shame though that our work came in handy for them. Our holes, the ones we dug. Where are you off to?"

"I'm going. Give it a try; why do you ask?"

"Why – because you'll get fined. We got fined 50 roubles the other day. I says to him: you might take for just the one, surely he couldn't count me and my daughter. You can't mean it? And he says: I'm letting her off (pointing to my grand-daughter), be thankful for that. Can you believe it? I scraped up 47 roubles for him. And still he asks where my daughter works, says he'll come there."

"Oh, that's rubbish, he won't."

"No, you see she works as a cashier. That's why he expects to get something."

The daughter: "It was porridge he was after. Eating is still a very important matter after all." (The little girl starts whim-pering and tugging at her grandmother: "Let's go, let's go!")

"No, we're not going, you just wait. After we've killed the Germans, then we can go where we like. After we've killed the Germans. Your grandad is chasing them away round Tula. Her grandad's there. As soon as I heard about Oryol, I felt a real lift. It means we've still got the strength . . ."

That's it – a real grandmother talking like a granny in the articles and stories. That's never happened before. Only in talk of the war does the language of the people merge with that of the newspapers.

*

The food mania, the maniacal conversations about it – all this intensified enormously during the "breathing space". During the days of the great hunger, people mostly kept quiet. Possibilities were cut off completely so there was no space left for psychological adornment of the bare facts or using the eternal human will for the affirmation of values.

Quantity of suffering turns into a different quality of sensation, in the same way that those who are badly wounded experience no pain in the first instant and those frozen to death fall into a pleasant state towards the end. Genuine hunger, as is well known, is not like the desire to eat. It has its masks. It used to display the face of misery, indifference, an insane urgency, cruelty. It most resembled a chronic disease, and as with any disease, the mind played a most important role. The doomed were not those with the blackest features, or those most emaciated or distended. They were the ones with the strange expressions, looks of weird concentration, the ones who started trembling in front of a plate of soup.

A used to arrive at the canteen with swollen dark red lips; and that wasn't the worst of it. On one occasion the salt had disappeared from the tables and the porridge was served out unsalted. At this A fell into despair. He rushed from table to table, mumbling: "Can't eat unsalted porridge . . . you just can't . . . Oh, good lord, and I didn't bring any . . ."

Now that was a bad sign.

B arrived at the canteen one day with a big lump torn out of the belly of his overcoat. He gave no explanation of this. He sat at table in this coat and chatted with his neighbours. One woman near him suddenly dropped a teaspoonful of sunflower oil from her porridge into one of the dirty dishes. "Waste not, want not," said B in a worldly-wise tone scooping up the oil in his own spoon, and eating it. About two weeks later he died in hospital.

During the civil war years it had been a different kind of starvation, elemental and chaotic (especially in the provinces).

They ate all sorts of fantastic things: vegetable peelings, rats and so forth, at the same time, mixing stuff together and making trades; then suddenly they'd get hold of a sack of potatoes. The siege starvation was a well-organized one. People knew that they would receive from somebody invisible the minimum ration, at which level some lived and some died – which it was depended on the organism.

The slowed-down people went on going monotonously to the bread shop and the canteen, awaiting the outcome. They were given the inevitable 125 grams of bread, a bowl of soup and saucer-sized portions of porridge. More than that it was impossible to buy, beg, borrow or steal. A friend and brother sat side by side clutching their 125 grams. No matter what agonies you were going through, you couldn't ask your best friend for any, and if he suddenly offered you some, you couldn't accept it, not if you were in your right mind.

Hamsun* described quite a different sort of hunger – that born from poverty, surrounded by hope and temptation. In that situation a man will suddenly find work or be given a loan, steal or beg something or have a decent pretext for dining with people he knows . . . The hungry yearnings of a poor man might be darkened by miscalculation, envy, humiliation but they had never before been crushed by inevitability.

In the spring the market was opened and the speculators gradually started creeping out. It turned out you could buy beetroot tops or even a glass of millet or peas – incredibly expensive and hard to find, but it was possible. The revival of the money factor was a mental revolution. Possibilities had appeared, and around these possibilities passions and interests began to come into play. It was from this time on that food started to become the focus of mental activity

* Knut Hamsun (1859–1952), Norwegian novelist and Nobel Prize-winner in 1920. He sprang to fame with his novel *Sult* (*Hunger*) in 1890.

(during the winter, if they spoke at all, it was about who was dying and how, not how they were eating). Food became a sphere of feasible activity and immediately took on various psychological refinements.

Against a background of universal, city-wide evolution, each person trod their own individual path – from incomprehension and frivolity to starvation-trauma. Moreover, the individual was subsumed into the group, into the typical reactions of the various strata of the population to the food tragedy.

Among these was the typical reaction of the '30s intellectuals, men and women, more or less young, with their pose of spending as little time and energy as possible on everyday matters. In that circle, one was allowed to be interested, not in food itself, but only in its psychological attributes: cosiness, relaxation, friendly conversation (accompanied by a glass of vodka), a projected supper with a girl. Otherwise, interest in food was considered to be a dependency of the lowest kind.

As the features of the siege began to grow clearer, intellectuals of this type went on glorying in their freedom from the lowest forms of dependency, from which stemmed, at first, a naïve misunderstanding of the famine. That is, they understood that there might be famine in the country, especially in the desert, complete with camels and mirages, when a man doesn't have anything to eat for days on end and dies in agony from that. But they knew nothing of dystrophy and didn't believe that the inhabitants of a large city could die of hunger.

N overlooked the beginning of the city's frightful calvary of famine – like many another, who coped with the increasing shortages with relative ease. He marvelled (he liked marvelling) when someone said: "This is it – starvation"; when a neighbour with a two-year-old child suddenly stopped coming down into the air-raid shelter, because they would certainly perish from hunger if the bombs didn't get them first

60

(she did in fact die in February). He enjoyed this surprise and incomprehension as the mark of a superior mind.

Then came the day when it became impossible to be ignorant any longer. People around were dying, though not in the way they died in the desert. On hearing of the first cases of deaths among their acquaintances, people still thought: Is this the one I know? In broad daylight? In Leningrad? With a doctorate? From starvation? They still talked and still recounted with horror how his wife in the last day, desperately trying to save her husband, bought a kilo of rice for 500 roubles.

Conversations gradually narrowed down to statements of fact. In the spring, talk branched out again, but during the winter this was too naïve an occupation. The average discussion centred on the bread ration and dinner. Worse – the dinner allotted to a man by the laws of the new dispensation was not his meal. According to the laws of the new dispensation, persons with a dependant's coupon were not permitted a meal, it did not guarantee a daily dinner. And a blockade person, registered at the official canteen, would divide it. He ate either just the soup, or just the porridge, or half of it. The rest he would take home in a milk can or a plastic box. It was odd to see a half-portion of porridge being carried home in gay blue and yellow boxes. Sharing was a sad business, and those who did so envied those who ate all of their dinner. There weren't many of the latter, however, especially to begin with, when the dependants had not died yet or hadn't got evacuated. The sharers were envious not so much of the satiety of the non-sharers, as of their unclouded enjoyment of the meal.

Once there were two men left at the table in an official canteen. One of them was holding a blue box in his hand and was gloomily shaking porridge into it from a spoon – the half-portion he had left uneaten on his plate. The other had already finished eating; he watched closely as the slippery

61

mush crawled down off the spoon. Then he suddenly said: "Ah, you can still share it, can you? I can't . . . You know, I can't share now . . ."

At that moment the sharer felt a flush of pride and strength.

N at length understood. But for him the worst came when it seemed things should have been easier: he was getting 400 grams then on his worker's ration card. Four hundred grams couldn't stave off emaciation, which was reaching the crisis-point. As soon as that point was reached – restraint began to break down. N suddenly began to eat everything he could immediately. At first this was without any planned intention, each time with a sense of sinfulness. Later on, he erected it into a principle.

With bread it went like this: early in the morning he would get his 400 grams and eat the make-weight pieces on the spot. He took the rest to the office, where he lived and worked on an oilcloth sofa because at home it was well below zero. In another of the vacant offices he seated himself at a desk and with a penknife pared off the first slice – approximating with his eye how much he was allowed to eat that morning. As the time approached the longing for bread intensified. He cut off another, thinner slice, breaking his limit. Then another one. This was accompanied by a sense of biblical fall. Then, when the limit had been irretrievably breached, an outlandish, horribly simple notion: what if he were to allow himself to eat it all, to the last crumb? He would freeze on the point of hesitation, then topple over. The illicit, hesitant delay was replaced by an irresistible slide downwards, eyes tightly closed. At the very instant when the ban was lifted he even had the fleeting illusion that now he didn't want to eat it all, that there was plenty of bread left; an illusion, needless to say, which vanished along with the next two or three slices.

A colleague gave N a pass for a canteen where they indulgently cut coupons out in advance and sometimes issued food

on the extra, usually voided coupons. The first time, when N had the idea of getting two main courses, it seemed almost incredible that it would happen. It was a revolution, an alteration in the principles of life. The increase in the bread ration or the amount of oats – that was remarkable, but the principle was unaltered – the principle whereby dinner was thought of as an enclosed, fixed entity. He couldn't break out and fit into himself an extra plate of soup.

There was, however, a situation in siege life which unlocked the circle for a time. This was when one of the family died and one could use their coupons till the end of the month.

In one of the corners of some office stood a woman, wrapped in headscarves. Her face dark and unmoving, she ate spoonful after spoonful of porridge out of a tin. By the standards of those days, there was quite a lot of porridge.

"My mother's died, you see," she stopped a passer-by she hardly knew, "the porridge is on her coupons . . . Such anguish, unimaginable anguish. And it won't pass, not for anything. I thought – what happiness to eat three bowls of porridge at once, four bowls . . . But I can't, I don't want it . . . I go on swallowing because the anguish, it's deep down, inside: I keep thinking it'll get better. This porridge, this mush will go down there inside and squash the anguish, cover it up or something. I eat, eat, but the anguish doesn't go away."

Towards spring people felt really bad, many of them worse than in the days of 125 grams (at that time their strength hadn't been sapped) but their state wasn't to be compared with anything else, it was like itself, a desire to eat . . . People passionately wanted to eat.

Recalling the winter, what N mostly remembered was not food or hunger, but chronic illness with its various symptoms, and the masks of hunger in general, its psychological disguises. And all this was less humiliating and bestial than what happened to him when things were starting to improve.

He felt hungry all the time. He cut out his ration coupons with the crazy light-mindedness which had become a routine with him. He raked three portions of porridge into his plate, to make it look more, then fell into despair because there was actually so little. Not only did he begin thinking about it, after thinking about nothing at all for long enough, but a maniacal concentration of thought possessed him completely. As he walked along the street he would recall slowly everything he had eaten that morning or the day before; he would ponder on what he was going to eat that day, or busy himself with calculations involving ration cards and coupons. He found in it an absorption and tension which he had previously known only when thinking through and writing something very important. A strange, warped reflection of intellectual activity – that was the most humiliating thing of all. And it seemed to him through a dystrophic haze, that this surrogate intellectual activity was altogether shameful, far more a matter for shame than any physiological functions. Unfortunately we don't realize it . . . or should it be fortunately?

On ration or shopping days, there were sometimes stocks at home. This even communicated a confident attitude to life. Busy about one's official duties, one could at any moment picture in all its ample solidity that tin on the second shelf, one third full of golden millet, in a nearby tin some silver sprats were neatly laid. Both the millet and the sprats were – beautiful.

Lots of people were still not at all ashamed. V the literary man used to say: "You know nowadays in bed, before I go to sleep, I amuse myself by compiling a lucky day's menu. For example: for breakfast, green porridge (out of beetroot tops) with bread, fried in paint-thinner; and tea with dried bread; lunch – two oat soups and millet porridge. Then at home, two cups of soya milk with a sweet (you can bring them back from the canteen); supper – green cake with soft

bread (because I have lunch without bread). Or breakfast: grated turnip from the market with vegetable oil; supper, baked soya sausage . . ."

Sometimes there were lucid intervals. Then you felt like gorging yourself to bursting point, till you were sick of the sight of food, to vomiting point – just so as to put an end to the shame, just to free your brain. But fear took hold of the dystrophic brain – what on earth would happen if it disappeared? If this complex of desires and goals were to resolve itself away?

What was it so sickeningly like? Something from the previous life? Ah, yes – being unhappily in love, when it was slowly releasing the bonds and you feared to lose along with it, not hope by now, not the emotion, but the guaranteed, accustomed filling of the vacuum.

One day, N could hold out no longer and as he was sitting at his editorial desk, muttered: "What matters now is – not to think about food."

There were two colleagues in the room, a man and a woman. The woman spoke swiftly: "I don't think about it."

"Liar," thought N.

The man said, smiling unpleasantly: "It's what we get for not being at the front. We have to pay some sort of price? Eh? Because we've been allowed to look after our precious lives."

"At the front, they don't think about food," thought N.

Towards the end of the winter, the rules of regulated existence relaxed. Various kinds of extra issues and purchaseable goods trickled through, soya milk, for example; later on there was a market with vegetable tops and nettles. The people who survived the winter best were those whose sense of self-preservation helped them to keep the destructive topic of food out of their minds. With the appearance of new possibilities, the protective prohibitions fell away and the mind was now exposed to the seductive element of food.

Food – in all its diversity of social genres, has been a subject of sublimation since time immemorial. We recall its ceremonial association with festivals and occasions, the rituals of reception and banquets, the significance of the family dinner in the everyday life of the landowner and bourgeoisie, the unfading significance of the supper for two.

Blockade people did not entertain one another. Food had ceased to be a medium of intercourse.

"I'm sorry I've come at an awkward time," X once said to Y, dropping in on business just at the moment when Y was frying some bread fritters on the stove. "I'm in your way. Food is a private matter nowadays."

Meanwhile X's face wore an odd inhuman expression. Yes, food had become an intimate and cruel business.

Human affairs always have their psychological aspect, however. After losing its psychological qualities, food quickly took on others. At one time a constituent part of the day's routine, it turned into the day's routine itself; once the accompaniment to events, it had become an event itself, simultaneously a sphere of social realization and naked gustatory sensations.

People accustomed to steak and hors d'oeuvres now discovered the taste of porridge, sunflower oil and oat fritters, not to mention bread. Imagination took wing in various directions – depending on the mentality involved. Some gave themselves up to the surrealist savour of roast goose or layer-cakes and sardines. Others dreamed of eating lots and lots more of what they were eating now. They wanted an unlimited prolongation of the same taste sensations. A restaurant serving grouse was an abstraction. This latter, however, a reality. But the imagination wanted to make this reality vast. This dream of quantity was not only a hyperbole of satiety, but also a struggle against despondency and fear in the face of the momentary, implacably transient existence of one's portion – even a double or triple portion.

People discovered a multitude of novel taste sensations, but nothing revealed so many as bread. That had been hitherto unexplored territory, the more so as many of the intellectual sections of society had not even been quite sure how much a kilo of black bread had cost before the war.

Some were possessed by bread mania in its purest form. Just bread, our daily bread . . . Others elaborated their fantasies about bread. They had an urge for example to sit in front of a dark loaf, cut thick slice after thick slice and dip it in sunflower oil. A.F. used to say he only wanted one thing – to drink sweet tea and buttered rolls for all eternity. A third group varied the bread theme. They thought about flour porridge sweetly gluing up the mouth, oat porridge and its gentle slimy feel.

In the spring, they were eating bread, fried and toasted. Thickly sliced crusts, toasted on the outside and left moist on the inside went especially well with tea. If you didn't snatch bread right from the frying pan with your fingers, but ate it with a knife and fork – then you had a *meal.*

Z told me how he had chanced to visit a privileged household in the course of business during the siege. Pouring out his tea, the lady of the house said: "You needn't go easy on the bread, you know. We've got more than enough."

Z looked at the bread basket and saw the impossible: ordinary, old-fashioned, pre-blockade bread. Unshared, unhoarded. The bread and buns were lying in uneven pieces among some smaller slices and crumbs. Moreover, the bun had had time to get hard.

Z went on eating, unabashed and without any particular hankering after the bread; he was assailed by disappointment. This measureless bread would have been appropriate in a dream, but in reality, it clearly required a different non-siege apperception.

By the spring, the dystrophic had gained in independence to the extent that he once more felt the urge to take pride in

himself and assert his identity. Some knew how to get hold of, distribute and cook food – and took pride in this, as a mark of superior strength. Others couldn't do all this and took pride in that as an indication of their superior spiritual organization. With the revival of the market, some started being proud of buying beetroot tops or nettles very cheaply, others that they spent money freely.

Getting on the academic ration, lunch without coupons, a parcel from unoccupied Russia, was like being promoted in your job, or getting a medal, or being praised in the papers. Moreover the hierarchy here revealed itself with unusual clarity and crudity. The Writers Union sometimes used to get parcels from Moscow now. They were amazing parcels – with chocolate, butter, rusks, tins of preserves and concentrates. The board decided how they were handed out. According to the roster in the possession of the man weighing out the butter, some writers who took an active part in union affairs got 1 kilo 800 grams, others got a kilo (those who were inactive got nothing at all from the parcels). Those who got the 1 kilo 800 grams felt ashamed of taking pride in the fact, but they couldn't help doing so. For those getting a kilo, the butter was poisoned. Many would have been happier with, say, 500 grams, as long as it was a testimony to their literary and public deserts.

The blockade person would return home with his booty. He carried it in his briefcase, lunch pail, string bag – bread on his first category card, off-ration soup, two or three turnips, which he had bought – that is, had the opportunity of buying at the price fixed by the speculators. The scholar would be carrying the half-loaves given to him for his lecture at the bread factory; the actor carries his suitcase with care; after his performance he was slipped several pieces of sugar, as intoxicating as a "full house" notice. A person carries his public recognition along with him.

There was an essential difference between those who lived alone – an ever-increasing number, as some members of

families died and others were evacuated – and those who had dependants, with their dependants' ration cards which did not stretch to daily soup.

The significance of dependants in the existence of the blockade person out hunting was twofold. It was fateful, often fatal, because the hunter had to share, and in sharing, lived in a perpetual hell of brutality, remorse, cruelty and pity. At the same time, they – those at home – were the last ethical factor in the situation, a social symbol close at hand. Here's one person carrying off his spoils, to swallow them down in silence in his lonely habitation. And here's another who will come home, lay out his catch on the table and find an ecstatic response.

Among the siege stories I have collected is the story of O, one of those who occasionally received his 1 kilo 800 grams of butter, along with rusks and concentrates. His sister had got stranded in Leningrad (she was a lot older than him). His sister's people had all perished and he was compelled to take her in – by now in an irreversible condition of dystrophy.

O was a person capable of rationalization and system. But in his siege existence, which he had tried to overcome by the rational direction of his will, his sister was the source of persistent recalcitrant disorder. He was irritated by her growing uselessness and the sacrifices he had made and continued to make for her sake. He told her of this with a roughness which astonished him. But immediately alongside this, there existed another layer of consciousness where it was obvious that without his sister, the silence would be final and beyond belief. And his former dreary recreations and amusements would be impossible. The processes of preparation and consumption of food were no longer the dark manipulations of a maniac; the presence of a second person brought him a touch of humanity. He looked at the woman, stumbling around the stove, with her little hands, prehensile and black, utterly unlike what they had been – and spoke roughly, by

now only because it had become a habit: "We're going to eat now. Set the plates out. Wipe it so we can sit down to a meal like normal people. Clear that dirty mess up . . ."

The dystrophic sister was an externalizing medium, an audience evaluating success – the concentrates and rusks, received because of his reasonably high position in the hierarchy.

Such was the siege story of O., a story of pity and cruelty . . .*

There were two basic systems in operation: some reckoned out their food over the whole day, others ate everything they could lay their hands on immediately. The first took precautions against themselves. They knew that enclosed food was the best protected – preserves, uncleaned herring, soya sausage with its skin unbroken. The second group affirmed that it was better to eat one's fill occasionally, than always be in a state of semi-starvation. The first took pride in their restraint and despised the second for their lack of discipline. The second were proud of their daring and audacity and regarded the first as a German student used to regard a philistine.

During the great hunger, the question was simple: Would a man eat his 125 grams straight away or in one or two goes? As things got easier, questions multiplied. Various kinds of food came into being and various emotional attitudes towards it.

The regular food was almost free and was paid for by precious coupons. Its psychological ambience was cruelty, limits which were not to be questioned. Therefore it evoked misery. There were other distributions: soya; soya milk; the well-known oilseed-cake (soya waste) which amazed those

* In earlier manuscripts, Ginzburg wrote instead of this line: "But to the blockade story [history] of O I will still return. To a story [tale] of pity and cruelty" (*"No k blokadnoi istorii O ia eshche vernus'. K rasskazu o zhalosti i o zhestokosti"*). The thumbnail sketch of O and his sister is a compression and transposition of the relationship between Otter and his aunt. See pages 137–210.

who visited Leningrad from unoccupied Russia or the front line; meatless bones (others had already eaten the meat) which people boiled up into brawn. This was optimistic food, a gift, a windfall and you could devour it at once with a feeling of righteousness.

Finally there was food for which you paid enormous sums (there were different kinds here too – the market and covert speculation). Attitudes to it were morbid and half-hearted. Logically there was no difference of course whether they tore off coupons, which didn't last to the end of the month anyway, or whether you ate groats* bought out of your budget at 600 roubles a kilo. But emotion and imagination could not be separated from that 600 roubles. And someone who could recklessly get through the food-issues and coupons was horribly afraid to overdo it when measuring out his single portion of purchased groats.

On the black market they paid 600–700 roubles for groats, and in the canteen porridge cost 15 kopecks. It was the weirdest feeling when a man, returning from the shop, suddenly realized that he was carrying bread worth 800 roubles and butter worth a thousand. That if he had declined that butter, the most inaccessible things would become his with the utmost ease.

The value of money now fluctuated – not in the abstract process of inflation, but tangibly, like during a card game (especially at night with chips). As long as the game goes on, money is weightless, its absolute value returns to it disagreeably in the morning.

Regulation food, off-ration or purchased food – it needed rationalization for it all to work together. Breakfast, for example, was in general built around bread, because that was easiest to get hold of in the mornings. On days when coupons

* The hulled and crushed edible grains of oats, and occasionally other cereals. Similar to American hominy grits made from maize.

71

were plentiful, one might get by without bread at lunch, but to do that you had to get to a second canteen where they gave you another two portions of porridge for coupons. If coupons were short then it was better to take your strict regulation dinner home and add some greens to the porridge – so you had to go to the market beforehand to get some vegetable tops. Bread didn't last till evening, so groats or flour bought from a profiteer was most often earmarked for supper.

Any failure was hard to come to terms with. It was impossible to go back to regarding food as belonging to the instant and vanishing with it. Nowadays there was a clear link between it and the human organism – and the life of that organism. A lost coupon, an off-the-ration issue missed – they couldn't be made up for with the possibilities of the following day. Nowadays it was an irreplaceable loss (a lost particle should have become a part of the organism and had not done so), and it could be forgotten only by someone who was light-minded and past remembering anything.

Intellectuals, especially, got carried away with rationalization, as they filled up their empty mental apparatus with new material. T, an out-and-out scholar, who had been unable out of principle to pour himself a cup of tea, now sat for hours, engrossed in reckoning up and allotting his coupons. He applied his powerful logical mind to the business. In general, during the period of the great hunger, the best organizers of the processes of satiety turned out not to be the housewives (they took up that responsibility in the spring again), but the people furthest from household management, especially men, who were free of routine and unsuited for day-to-day siege existence. Especially those same intellectuals who had all their lives feared to lay a finger on a besom or a frying pan, thinking it would cast doubt on their manhood – when in actual fact, the more courageous the man, the more naturally and simply he carries out non-male tasks (a soldier

has to know how to boil porridge and sew a button on). They don't run into any complexes over it.

The siege cooking mania took hold of the most unlikely people. Once I happened to observe a boy of 16 (the age of greatest contempt for womens' affairs) frowning and biting his lip as he baked some oatcakes. At once his mother came fussing round: "Let me . . . you don't know how . . ." But without a word he pushed her roughly away from the stove.

The more meagre the raw material involved, the closer it approached mania. All the maniacal activity stemmed from a single premise: just eating was too simple, left too little trace. Siege cookery resembled art – it conferred tangibility on things. Above all, every product had to cease being itself. People made porridge out of bread and bread out of porridge; they made cakes out of greens, and cutlets out of herrings. Elementary materials were transformed into dishes. These efforts at cookery were motivated by the thought that it was tastier or more filling that way. But it wasn't that, it was the pleasure of fiddling about, the enriching of the lingering, protracted process . . .

Sometimes there was an issue of tobacco (smoking was a good suppressor of hunger). Everyone rolled their own. Here the same principle obtained of pleasurable lingering. To sprinkle tobacco dust into paper, roll it up, lick it, stick it in a holder – this was both a foretaste and a voluptuous handling of a precious substance.

In papirosy, on the other hand, when they became available, there was something disappointing and flat – too simple, too all-at-once.

The hungry impatience which drove a person homewards, compelled him, before taking off his coat and galoshes, to rush over and stoke up the stove – impatience subsided somehow when the bustle with the actual food items began. In these moments a person thought less of his hunger than at

any other time: he was distracted by his impassioned interest in what was taking place.

The wife of Professor P spoke timidly: "There's your pasty falling to bits. Why make pasties out of it?" she had in mind millet porridge. "Let's just eat it the way it is . . . It's all right even when it's cold."

He cried out in despair: "You've got no idea, have you? No idea! Toss that firewood over here this minute!"

The cooking technique of literary men and associate professors was accompanied by vast disorder, stemming from their haste and dilettantism. The dilettante scorches his face as he bends down to the open hatch of the stove to throw in another small log. With the other hand he stirs about in the pan. The pan should be moved off now and replaced by the kettle, because things only heat up properly in the centre, especially where the stove has heated right through. At the same time you have to keep an eye on the toasting bread, so that the dark golden-brown crust isn't covered in black sooty spots. The dilettante finds even sooty and greasy hands a positive pleasure.

Chaos mounts around him. Unaccountably there are three spoons, and first one, then another finds its own way into his hand. The pan lid has turned up in the empty frying pan on the floor. Shapeless cloths hang on the stovepipe, the chair back, the basket of firewood. He thinks he is picking up the right implement every time and using it in the proper manner. But things drift off into chaos. Still, it is a friendly chaos, smelling of food and warmth.

Intellectual chefs, for all their inventiveness, used to spoil their work because they just couldn't let the cooking food well alone. They were forever lifting the lids, mixing and turning over. Some dishes were interesting from this point of view, while others were boring. Soup, for example, was very dull. It boiled away tediously for ages and nothing else happened to it really. Visual changes were diverting on the

other hand. Porridge swelled up and grew (marvellous how it increased in quantity), then began to snuffle and breathe underneath the light steam seething above it. Dumplings fell from the spoon into the boiling water and came to pirouetting life in the new element – it was almost like a conjuring trick. Flat cakes might fall grotesquely to pieces, or might take on streamlined form immediately.

It was delicious to rub a spoon along the bronze-coloured liquid pastry made for dumplings or fritters, and the temptation was to lick it, like chocolate cream.

The intellectual chef would suddenly freeze amid his manipulations. There came the flickering transient thought that all this was horribly reminiscent of something. Love, was it? . . . La Rochefoucauld asserted that love was the need for a roundabout way to the desired end.

N – one of the intellectual siege chefs – eventually prepares to have breakfast. By the table, pushed closer to the stove, he meticulously cuts a slice of bread into small squares. They are destined to be placed in boiling water and mashed with a spoon. As a boy he had sometimes watched the girls playing when he was at the dacha. They were playing at dinner and making flat cakes out of grass and pasties of sand. He watched these female games contemptuously, but he was bored and he gradually moved closer and joined in with an indifferent expression. As the man, he was allotted the heavy work – cutting firewood with his penknife and fetching water from the stream in a pail. The game began to draw him in and soon he was alongside the girls, raptly converting the sand into pastry and the grass into filling. Virtually what he was doing now.

The day was organized nowadays around three focal points: breakfast, lunch and supper. Everything that happened at home or shop from five or six in the morning onwards, was geared towards the first of these. And every time something went wrong at the climactic moment. After

everything that N, from the moment he awoke, had done for this breakfast, after he had seated himself with a certain solemnity at the table, having first wiped it with a cloth, he ate everything in absent-minded haste, though he knew that now his food should be appreciated and savoured. He wanted to say, but couldn't: *Verweile doch! Du bist so schön!**

Just like in the former life when the relentless instants bore away everything of his mental and emotional experience, suffering and happiness, effort and sacrifice. As he breakfasted, N recalled the siege theory concerning the enjoyment of food. No, today it was pointless, now that almost everything had been eaten . . . I'll try next time . . .

But next time the moment could not be arrested either.

In the winter the desire to eat was like a disease; satiety represented the ending of an illness. Therefore the renewal of the desire to eat after a few hours or the following morning was received with a kind of astonishment and distress. Like one's temperature rising again or the return of pain on swallowing when you thought the angina had passed off.

Nowadays people experience hunger less often, but are constantly striving to stave it off. That is precisely why they experience it less often. Less often in fact than in pre-siege times when it had seemed natural, even pleasant – when you were waiting for your lunch.

Nowadays, however, blockade people have already started to say (especially before eating): "I'm hungry as a beast, I'm hungry as hell." These are peace-time phrases. They didn't talk like that during the winter. It would have seemed unthinkable, a shameless frankness of appetite. The return of these phrases is a sign of recovery. But people aren't used to them yet. They still surprise speaker and listener every time. How is it possible, just like that, coming out with those

* Stay! Thou art so fair! (Goethe: *Faust*).

76

terrible words like in the old days? They denote suffering and despair – not at all an appetite for lunch.

The well-fed do not understand the hungry, themselves included. Once having eaten his fill, a man gradually lost his understanding of himself – the way he had been in the months of the great hunger . . . The blockade people forgot their sensations but they remembered facts. Facts slowly crept out from the dimness of memory into the light of behavioural rules which were gravitating by now towards the accepted norm.

". . . She wanted a sweet so much. Why did I eat that sweet? I could have not eaten that sweet. And everything would have been just a little bit better . . ."

Thus a blockade person thinks about his wife, mother, whose death has made the eaten sweet irrevocable. The mists of dystrophy disperse and the one alienated from himself comes face to face with the objects of his shame and remorse. For those who survived the siege, remorse was as inevitable as the malnutrition changes in the organism. In its grimmest form too – *uncomprehending* remorse. A person recalls the fact but cannot summon up the experience: the experience of that piece of bread, or sweet, which had prompted him to cruel, dishonourable, humiliating deeds.

. . . And the screaming over those millet cutlets . . . burnt . . . The screaming and despair, to the point of tears . . .

Perhaps he will again be able to sit in a restaurant after dinner, morose after a too-ample meal, which has induced a mood of cheerlessness and a disinclination to work. Perhaps while waiting for the bill, his eye lights on the bread basket, with its dark and white slices. And this almost untouched bread suddenly galvanizes his dulled consciousness with a shudder of recollection.

Pity is the most destructive of the passions and unlike love and anger, it never passes.

Tolstoy (in *Reminiscences*) wrote about his auntie Yergolskaya, how nice she was and how he could never recall without a pang of conscience how sometimes (being very short of money) he had refused her money for the sweets she loved to keep by her, only so that she would have something to offer him as a treat. She used to sigh sadly. "And I refused her of all people that small pleasure . . ."

The dystrophics who survived would have given a lot for landowner conscience-pangs like this.

The circle was the siege symbol of consciousness closed in on itself. How to break through it? People run round the circle and can't run their way to reality. They think they're at war, but it isn't so – it's those in the front line who are at war. They think they're not at war, but just keeping themselves alive, but that's not true either, because they're doing what has to be done in this fighting city, to prevent the city from dying.

That is the way with people whose activities are not actions but reactions. How to break the circle with a deed of some sort? A deed is always an acknowledgment of common ties (without which one can only moan and groan), ties that are binding on a person even in spite of himself, though egocentrics go on and on and always will (on a world scale) about self-deception, the absurd and the impossibility of contact.

Those who write, whether they will it or no, enter into a conversation with what is outside the self. Because those who have written die, but that which was written remains behind, without asking their permission. Perhaps it would be the simplest thing of all for the isolated consuousness to do without posthumous social existence, with all its compulsory benefits. Perhaps, deep down it would prefer to be annihilated completely, along with all it contains. But

those who have written die, whereas what has been written remains.

To write about a circle is to break the circle. A deed whichever way you look at it. In the abyss of lost time, something found.*

<div align="right">1942–1962–1983</div>

* Ginzburg's phrase (in Russian: *V bezdne poteriannogo vremeni – naidennoe*) makes clear reference to Marcel Proust, and therefore one could alternatively translate "found" as "regained", as in the title *Le Temps retrouvé (Time Regained)*, the final volume of *In Search of Lost Time*. Proust was one of the most important writers for Ginzburg. She wrote in one of her essays from the early 1960s: "After Hegel, it seems, no one has defined art as powerfully as Proust. In the last volume he explained why art is needed, and by the same token, why it has existed and will continue to exist. Art is time regained, it is a battle with nonbeing, with the horror of not leaving a trace. Objecthood regained, for every object can bring time to a stop. The creative spirit has won its greatest victory – it has stopped the river into which it is impossible to step twice."

Around *Notes from the Blockade**

Notes during the Siege

One ought not to think that everything altered radically. Of course the material elements changed, but much of the mechanics continued to function through sheer inertia. Meanwhile, everybody wanted change, and expected psychological changes to take place.

Thinking about "how it would be" (which is what everybody was thinking about . . .) we continually miscalculated, ascribing too much significance to the mortal danger factor. It turned out to be simpler just to go to the front line than to halt the mechanisms. It was an unequal choice between danger close at hand, certain and familiar (the management's displeasure) and the outcome of something as yet distant, unresolved, and above all, incomprehensible.

The boundary between lies and truth became blurred, the truth of those who, perhaps, would not have been averse to extricating themselves, but once having found themselves in a war situation, conducted themselves strictly according to its rules, the truth of boys, who simply considered that they

* The title in Russian introduces a pun. The circle (*krug*) is a central symbol of the blockade (the blockade encircles the city, N's routines go in circles), and Ginzburg's addenda to her original work is "around" or "surrounding" *Notes from the Blockade.*

ought to go as soon as possible; such boys were legion. Here is a letter (June 1941) by one 18-year-old, preserved by the woman to whom it was addressed:

Irina, hello!
I am going to be witness to something extraordinary and significant – I'm off to the front! Do you realize what that means? Oh no, you can't possibly.

It's a trial of yourself, your views, tastes, qualities. And that's not a paradox – perhaps I'll be able to understand Beethoven better, and the genius of Lermontov and Pushkin, once I've been at war.

Well, there's no time to write. Well, now I feel superior to you. I am going to have the opportunity of plunging into the vortex of life, while you, you are doomed to swot away at your old scholasticism – too bad!

About the "scholasticism" was I exaggerating?
Never mind. Perhaps we'll meet sometime, eh?
I squeeze your hand ever so hard.
 Oleg

They did not meet. Oleg was killed very soon after.

They said about Okudzhava's story* ("Good Luck, Schoolboy") that it portrayed a coward, a sniveller, a mental deserter, and nobody noticed the curious fact that this wretched boy, who was afraid, and sorry for himself, and wants his mother to be sorry for him – not once, not for an instant did he doubt that he had to go and carry out his terrible task.

* Bulat Shalvovich Okudzhava (1924–97): poet and writer, who volunteered for the front in 1942. He made his reputation in the 1960s, accompanying his poetry on the guitar. His story "Good Luck, Schoolboy" appeared in 1961. He is also the author of several novels, including *The Closed-Down Theatre,* which won the 1994 Russian Booker Prize.

The fear of the habitual and understood (for example, the fear of violating current norms of behaviour) is stronger than the fear of the unknown, or at least quicker to manifest itself; this is the reflex that comes into play first. It is the condition which enables the mental norm to be preserved right up to the moment when deadly danger grips the emotions and becomes an all-engrossing experience of terror or ecstasy.

How far are such states of mind from the normal person? How prominent are they in mental existence? In Tolstoy's opinion, they were well in the background; his psychology of war is in fact based on that.

The human mind is not permitted to conceive of the disappearance of that mind; as is well known, this has given rise to extremely complex systems of suppression and displacement in order to render that notion harmless. The terminology has changed but the revelation of a suppression system goes back a long way through the ages; thinkers from La Rochefoucauld to Freud and the existentialists have reiterated it. The war to some extent paralysed this system; on the other hand, it also to some extent created pretexts for it: social suppression of personal desires and goals, powerful ideological and emotional stimuli, force of habit, nervous elation or the indifference of dystrophy.

In Leningrad, people revealed so little physical cowardice on the whole, that it was unable to paralyze other weaknesses and vices. For example, the classic squabbling assembly – under artillery bombardment, in a building that happened to have been hit already. One of the editorial department heads had been sacked and sent to a front-line paper. His successor – a nice person – goes through the whole ritual: censure of the former management (there's also the article in the wall newspaper signed: Pegasus), self-justification in the form of self-criticism, a nod in the direction of comrades promoted by his predecessor. A writer with a personal grievance (in military uniform) plays an opening move "I cannot

keep silent . . ." on the subject of, in the given instance, poorly qualified editors, who "have still not learned . . ." Is there anything here that bears any relation to the whistling and the regular explosions? Yes – the supplementary phraseology. "Now more than at any other time . . ."

The continuing activity of these mechanisms was especially striking in cases where lost ration cards were restored or rather not restored. The loss of ration cards was a mass phenomenon – clearly a consequence of exhaustion and over-taxed nerves. The system involved a weird combination of the old (bureaucratic) form and new content (people dying of hunger). The secretaries were all alike, traditional.

For instance, there is a sadistic type quite widespread among administrative personnel. This is the malicious secretary. If she were to be set down in a canteen to cut out coupons, she would take pleasure in telling you that you couldn't have a second helping of porridge, or that this coming week – how odd you didn't know – you haven't got a single groats coupon left. If she is placed where people go who have lost their ration books, she talks to them in a loud voice with the studied tones of rejection, gently restraining her administrative triumph.

Then there is the languid secretary, with beautiful heavily made-up eyes, not yet dressed siege-fashion. She is preoccupied with her own thoughts. She regards you without malice, her only desire to rid herself of an inconvenience, and rejects you lazily, even a little plaintively (complaining about the inconvenience). There is, finally, the businesslike woman. For some women, the fact of being occupied in an important public capacity has not yet become second nature (a curious atavism). They savour their efficiency, to the boundless irritation of those around them. Women doctors of this propensity, when talking to an intellectual patient, love to explain their prescriptions, translating from Latin to Russian on the spot, and saying: "We call this . . ."

If the malicious secretary finds in her work a source of power-loving enjoyment, if for the languid secretary work is a necessary concession to reality, the businesslike woman prizes the official process itself. She turns you down majestically, but circumstantially, with sermonizings and reasons. And although she is only interested in what she is saying, the person who will likely be dead in a few days without a ration card is comforted for a moment by these reasons. Squabblers and secretaries, angry officials and outraged writers – all these have retained their forms and functions in some strange way. In Tolstoy's view, this stability of selfish interests and inveterate custom was objectively necessary. It was an indication that the whole existed, that the numberless aspirations are, as before, bound together in a single knot. Would the business of the country and the war have been done differently and better without squabblers and officials? Of course. But the whole could not get rid of them with the war going on. It had other things to do.

Under the artillery bombardment, the mechanisms of social evil went on functioning normally alongside heroism and fortitude. This tortured land was winning. And was, without realizing it, preparing to enter a new debauch of social evil.

Utopian thinking did not wish to recognize that social evil is ineradicable (though it can be substituted), that humankind has had its replacers of evil. Sometimes these were the most appropriate, progressive, so to speak, substitutes. But still . . . if you grumble about social evil – be sure that it doesn't occupy the place of something still more lethal. As distinct from social hedonism, religion does not exorcise evil and does not promise to wipe it out (or only in the kingdom of heaven); it incorporates it into its system of two worlds – this one and the next. As far as the next one is concerned . . . it's a matter of getting one's due. For the rest, the most vital problem is how, without religion, to escape egoism. What is that citzenship, that love, that lofty toil which will furnish a means of avoiding the infernal misery of egoism?

85

The egoist is like a savage. The primitive mind is filled with terror at the hostility of the world. It is vanquished by culture – a hierarchical chain of values – by creativity, which makes what is one's own other, and by love, which makes what is other one's own.

As a system of values breaks down, the cultured man undergoes a second primitivization. As his existence crumbles, he takes on caveman ways, a caveman's attitude to fire, to food, to clothes. The egoistic man wanders blindly among phenomena which are either aggressively or indifferently hostile, searching for a loophole involving the least evil for himself. The actual bearers of the greatest evil, taking upon themselves its theoretical analysis, are standing outside the gates. We all want to kill them; we want to kill as many as possible, without going into the details of their human existence at all. As he reads in the paper about fascist arms and legs flying into the air, the intellectual feels satisfaction.

The varieties of evil mingle in an odd fashion; though separate from one another, they work as one. As they passed through the yard with buckets of rubbish or buckets to fill with water in the slippery laundry, people would eye a large lock on the doors of the block office. It had a reassuring look. The '60s generation won't understand that. Nowadays, block managers look after their blocks and their residents with more or less success. In the '30s they existed for quite a different purpose, perhaps not altogether clear even to themselves. Not only to keep an eye on the inhabitants; more to remind each inhabitant hourly, that everything he proposed, even in his private existence, might be halted, taken away, forbidden. They were Stalin's advance guard . . . And here was this evil under heavy lock and key; the dystrophic block manager could no longer get to his office. The dialectics of the varieties of evil.

*

Suffering and death on a large scale was never the exclusive mark of war; epidemics and natural disasters engulf entire cities. What particularizes war is the combination of these possibilities with an extreme lack of freedom, open, loudly declared, dispensing with the need for camouflage.

Bourgeois democracies always doubt the right of state laws to demand of the free man that he should not get behind a steering wheel when drunk, but never doubt the right of the state in certain circumstances to demand a man's life and in the event of his deserting, try him as a traitor. The world was horrified at Mao's suggestion of exterminating half the world's population so that the remaining half might build a beatific state on the ruins of capitalism. What is novel and frightening in this project, however, lies essentially in the quantitative factor. Not long ago, President Johnson said in a television speech: "We grieve over those killed (in Vietnam) on both sides (he might have left the other side in peace), but there is no power which could make the USA shrink from the cause of freedom and justice." This logic is no different from Mao's except that one case involves half mankind and the other an indeterminate number of American lives. From the individualistic point of view it matters not at all that a million people perish, what matters is that one person dies a million times. Mao's logic is the necessary logic of a state (capitalist, bourgeois-democratic included); it is merely Asiatic in its baldness and scale.

Absolute unfreedom can appear to a man psychologically as some new aspect of public life or, on the other hand, simply a further development of his normal burdens and misfortunes. In the recognizability of misfortune lie the strength and weakness of anti-individualistic structures.

Here we have a person brought up in the hedonistic illusions and camouflaged forms of compulsion. Something that commands, forbids, curtails and regulates his creature comforts – all this is exotic to him, a new quality, born of

an extraordinary situation, which demands the summoning up of all spiritual and physical powers. He even imagines his permission has been asked and he consequently regards his actions as a *deed*. And deeds have a psychological aura of their own – one of pride and vanity, selflessness and passion.

On the other hand there are those for whom there is nothing in all this that is new in principle. Some react by attempting to escape, others with tremendous fortitude. Sometimes there are attempts at evasion to begin with and great fortitude later. However this may be, for them it is just the latest phase in their age-old relationship with Leviathan. This name, that of the mighty monster celebrated in the book of Job, was that given by Hobbes to the all-powerful state. Leviathan possesses various kinds of wards: those who think the same, those who think differently and those who don't think at all. Their mutual relationships take various social and psychological forms. A coincidence of aspirations, conscious or instinctive is possible; resistance is possible, also conscious or instinctive. A combination of absolute power and the absolute egoism of the person subject to it shows us a peculiar, theoretically valuable aspect of social psychology. They are attached to one another and at the same time, impervious to one another.

There are many gradations here too – from the position of the snob, with his illusions of inner independence, to the condition of the slave, the most egoistic state of all. Who is more egoistical than a rower permanently chained to the hull of a galley? Every objective element of life is taken from him; all that is left to him is his suffering body. The egoism of slaves is overshadowed by the intensity of their suffering and the paltriness of their desires and goals, but it is, essentially, limitless.

The immanent person, estranged from absolutes and universal values, has existed as a mass, socially typical figure in various guises, at different stages of society. Here I will

speak only of his intellectual manifestation. I have in mind the consciousness which came about in the Russia of the 1880s, taking over from the *narodnik** tradition. It produced not only sworn positivists, but also decadents (an experiment in the pure culture of egoism) and in the final analysis, the symbolists, with their romantic attempt to seize the objective through the subjective, and much that followed with or without orienting itself towards objective meaning.

It was Blok[†] who, with great intelligence and perception, linked positivism and decadence, in spite of their apparent differences. Blok realized that they were connected by way of their shared subjectivism and agnosticism. This consciousness presented a paradox: in its intellectual capacity it was supposed to develop values and ideals, meanwhile, being positivist and subjective it closed off the very springs from which values and ideals are derived.

After the First World War, western intellectuals were possessed by the aesthetics of disintegration, the denial of life and so on (the lost generation). With us, many of that stratum became fellow-travellers[‡] at first – so as to leave themselves the possibility of participation in public life, but also as a result of the age-old (from Herzen to Blok) Russo-intellectual

* The *narodniki* ("populists") were members of a radical utopian socialist movement existing between the 1870s and 1890s. The failure of their educational efforts among the peasantry in the 1870s led to the disillusion described in Turgenev's *Virgin Soil*. Extremists formed terrorist groups and Tsar Alexander II was assassinated by one of these (the People's Will).

† Aleksandr Aleksandrovich Blok (1880–1921): the leading poet of Russian Symbolism – also a playwright and essayist – whose influence on twentieth-century Russian poetry was colossal.

‡ A term used in the 1920s (into the early 1930s) to describe writers and intellectuals who were neither in the Communist Party nor directly opposed to it: instead they searched sometimes hesitatingly, for what Ginzburg called "points of compatibility" with the Revolution and the regime.

hatred of the old world. The fellow-travellers used to talk with lofty naïveté: "Now this of yours is good, and this is bad; we'll accept it from here to here . . ." and they were treated carefully. Later on, these former fellow travellers were to shout: "Genius!", abasing themselves, and they were methodically destroyed.

From 1914 began the era of great experiments and trials. The life-stance adopted by those of immanent sensibility demanded at least a minimum of creature comforts. Only under those conditions could philosophy take place, beginning with the sentence: But does life have meaning? The poverty-stricken egoist at once finds, if not the meaning of life, then an interest, goal, task – to survive. But he loses all his finery in so doing and is left looking terribly naked.

In wartime (the extreme of unfreedom) the egoistic man stumbled on a strange, shifting freedom – in the blurring of the bounds between open and covert forms of compulsion. Does it matter if someone has failed to make use of some rights or benefits, if the upshot is the same – or if the upshot is actually worse when the rights and benefits are greater? Who are the winners then, and who the losers? Where are the careerists and the establishments where they were making their careers? There stand their looted apartments, while their owners are borne off along the roads of war. What difference is there between published and unpublished books – if there are neither authors nor readers? And what have we to do with the catastrophic denouement of the age-old drama of individualism, when there is nobody to think about it and no time to do so. We have other concerns.

If the first experience of world war evoked a sharply individualistic intellectual reaction in Euro-American writers, then the second could only demonstrate its untenability. (Woe to the egoists and hedonists! There is nothing so frail and defenceless in this world.) The ineradicability of social evil and the illusory nature of the individual sensibility

was revealed twice and thrice to a shattered generation. Simultaneously came the collapse of two great delusions, seemingly contrary but in fact having a common origin in nineteenth-century humanism.

A man who is being tested to destruction by catastrophes is incapable of believing in beauty and the absolute value of the individual soul. It is much more natural for him to feel revulsion for that naked soul and a bitter futile longing for purification in the universal, some sought-for system of association – in religion? In existential self-projection? In a new citizenship?

The sense of community exists – conscious or unconscious, strong or weak, erected into a religious dogma or tentative because of its own illogicality. People receive this primary element of their own social structure, along with all the sign systems, which make up their cultural consciousness, together with language (i.e. thinking) – as a bearer of common meanings. A person accepts this enormous communal content, in order, through his own precarious life, to bring about changes, great or small; ultimately they are small compared with the totality.

This is why the communal sense is as real as the desires of egoistic emotions, often brutally intense, which mingle with it – mingle indeed in the same person (it depends on the socio-historical situation whether the nutritive medium favours one or the other). Even when acting egoistically, a person is inclined at the same time to evaluate actions – especially those of others, sometimes his own – according to communal norms. Communal norms, incidentally, by no means always invoke humanism – even in its official, camouflaged phraseology. The cruelty and self-interest of the collective also demand sacrifices from the individual, even total sacrifice (as demonstrated by fascism).

Either this sense of community seems to us an illusion, a mirage, opposed to logic, or the individual personality does.

Probably both of them taken separately are illusory; the reality of our experience is their reciprocity.

The history of the existentialists is characteristic of western European thought in the second quarter of the century. They were quick to load the personality *in its existence* with the burdens of the supra-personal. Some by way of a religious justification of life (when there's a god the justification is there in advance). Others through the ethics of the French Resistance.

Camus wrote his superb novel *The Outsider,* superb in the classical clarity of its conversation about life.* At the same time he wrote a philosophical commentary to that novel, *The Myth of Sisyphus*, short but complex (just like his *The Rebel*) in which there are certain inconsistencies.

The best thing in this tract is the epigraph from Pindar: *O mon âme, n'aspire pas à la vie immortelle, mais épuise le champ du possible.*†

In *The Outsider*, the fundamental principle of consciousness is pointlessness; chaos stirs; incomprehensibility, striking the man abandoned in it with horror. Beyond that is the sensory envelope of the life accessible to us. The first step in its justification. Here Camus stopped in the novel, while in the tract he went on to make a logically unsuccessful further step to a heroic affirmation of existence. What caused that step to fail was its denial of the obvious – the hierarchy, the network of social values which is laid down over incomprehensible chaos and the confusion of sensory experience. This is the second step in the justification of life. There is yet a third – absolutes . . . But that doesn't apply to us.

Without a hierarchy of values, what can be the objection if someone declares: "Well then, try to prove the obligatory

* *The Plague*, on the other hand, is an allegory. If you want to speak of fascism, why talk about a plague?
† O my soul, seek not immortality, exhaust rather the field of the possible.

nature of the moral demands made on me." The chief argument then against the practice of egoism is its frailty, its inability to protect a person.

As for the philosophy of egoism and hedonism, it is just glaringly inappropriate to our times. Something quite different was needed – the naïveté of a slave-owning society, perhaps? The abstraction of their enlightenment? The beautiful souls of the utopians or the satiety of the aesthetes?

Camus with his admonition addressed to the intellectuals: "I am saying to you – tomorrow you will be called up!" – is a man of the French Resistance. The collaborator Giono* proposed a different formula (it created a furore): "Better a living coward than a dead hero." Logical? Logical. But logic here is in urgent need of further elaboration. Actually it's a variation on the biblical theme of the living dog and the dead lion. What is left to us then is to aspire to the condition of the dog, the condition of animality, solitary pleasures and unmemorable sufferings. Whoever says: a living dog is better than a dead lion, must say: a living dog is also better than a living lion – that is, happier. This is in fact the idea of Ecclesiastes: "A living dog is better than a dead lion . . ." Not the dog is better, it is better for the dog.

The lion is brave, and a readiness for death is inherent in the make-up of the lion. The bald principle of extending life (any life) and the intensification of sundry pleasures is logically possible only when culture is rejected; this is because culture is a social fact and replaces the category of pleasure with the category of value. And the concept of value presupposes payment. Social man lives by the risky act of personally realizing the communal. Freedom, the homeland, science, art, love, the family, honour – all these are extremely

* Jean Giono (1895–1970): French novelist, author of more than 50 volumes, including the Pan trilogy (*Colline*, *Un de Baumugnes* and *Regain*), *The Hussar on the Roof* and *The Man Who Planted Trees*.

dangerous things. Sacrifice here is merely the condition of use. Hemingway's *For Whom the Bell Tolls* is about this. After all no one questions the conditions placed before airmen, motorcyclists or climbers.

I can't recall who said in answer to various medical warnings: "Living is dangerous – people die of it."

The intellectuals wanted to change. In the dismay of the first few days they wanted to be rid of loneliness, an egoism which intensified fear. It was an instinctive movement, which had a lengthy intellectual prehistory: the eternal dream of escape from the self, of responsibility, of the supra-personal. It all found absurd expression in an odd feeling of coincidence. The intellectual now had to want for himself the thing that the community wanted from him. The old utopian problem (how it exercised Herzen!) – could it not be resolved through a synthesis between the logic of the state and the logical absurdity of the personality as a value in itself?

Those not liable for call up urgently wanted to do something – go to the hospital, offer one's services as an interpreter, write an article for the paper, seemingly without wanting to be paid. These intentions and wishes fell into a machine that was totally unadapted to such psychological material. With customary rudeness and mistrust towards the good will of its wards, it threw people out of some sections and dragged them into others against their will.

Some days later there was an announcement through the Writers Union that everybody would be proceeding in an unknown direction to dig anti-tank ditches or build barbed wire entanglements. Some set off at once in search of medical certificates, others – the more intellectual, spoke contemptuously of people who at such a moment considered themselves above physical labour.

"And you know what physical labour is?" said Maximovich, recently returned from the camps. "Have you ever tried it?

94

Digging with your spade knowing that what you're doing is a long way below the norm. Ugh, these intellectual drivellers . . . Digging out earth is agony especially when it's absolutely useless. Well, you'll find out . . ."

They found out. The number of medical certificates rose swiftly. In fact the authorities soon stopped insisting. The mechanism worked formally, it treated a person according to the category he was in at any one time, or rather, his social status. In Leningrad, writers, artists and suchlike – were in the category of militia volunteers to begin with. Untrained and practically unarmed they were immediately thrown against fresh German forces. They all perished. Fairly soon, writers, artists and scientists became the gold star reserve category, who had to be evacuated and preserved. At first Shostakovich* was sent onto the roof to put out incendiaries, then he was brought out of Leningrad by special aircraft. They took great pride in both things. Soon the demands made on writers and so on were the same as they had always been, only more so.

The front line lived by its own laws. There were problems which someone resolved or didn't resolve, or the expectation of such problems. The deep rear also had its arrangements. They made guns or bread there; they were frankly just sitting it out. Just behind the lines, however, that part of the rear which was under fire, where there was practically nothing to be done (by civilians), a strange reality was established, in some ways resembling that of 1937.†

* Dmitry Dmitrievich Shostakovich (1906–75): the pre-eminent composer of twentieth-century Russian music. He lived and worked in Leningrad almost all his life, only leaving when he was evacuated from the city in 1941.
† This year is regarded as the most intense period of the Soviet purges of the 1930s.

Both the present and the past had their timetables.* The present ones flew in at strictly fixed times; German precision became part of the psychological assault ("we do what we want"). The past ones had been less meticulous; it was reckoned however, that after four in the morning they rarely came. From around four in the morning until evening you could imagine yourself safe. This imaginary breathing space probably saved a great many from going mad.

In the mute darkness – the expectation of frenzied ringing, or the series of interconnected sounds which presaged an air raid. The morning uncertainty . . . Gradually it becomes clear – a direct hit on the corner house. It gradually became clear that during the night so and so of your acquaintances had been arrested. Formerly they used to bomb the centre heavily, Mokhovaya for example or tried to hit the Radio building. But now, you notice, they're obviously interested in the Vyborg side.† Note how they've been avoiding the centre for ten days now. Maybe we'll get no more in the centre. Well, obviously it's a frame-up but why that frame-up? No accident. A was connected with such people . . . B was imprudent, he talked too much. C has these relatives, you know. If you didn't have relatives and didn't talk too much, maybe nothing would happen. They were leaving the centre alone at all events. Well, of course, the odd chance hit . . . A hit-and-miss system that clouded reason.

Can one live when they're 15 kilometres away? Or when you don't know in the evening where you'll meet the morning? But society lived on, throwing up appropriate forms of existence.

* In the Russian Ginzburg uses plural demonstrative pronouns (*U tekh i etikh byli svoi sroki* or literally "Those ones and these ones both had their timetables") to represent the present evil forces (the Germans), and the past ones (the secret police). Ginzburg's language here is purposefully vague.
† A northwestern section of Leningrad (currently St Petersburg) across the Neva River from the city centre.

The unfreedom of war is most intelligible of all when it achieves regulation. Just behind the lines the civilian does not work, or works only in a formal sense (the remaining factories and medical institutions are militarized to a greater or lesser extent) because there's nothing for him to produce. The siege left the unneeded person to get on with his own self-preservation. It was allowed, legalized.

"What do you do?" they asked Professor R, who had got stranded in Leningrad during the siege winter. He responded: "I eat."

Strange, augmented reflection of that former reality, its unfreedom and its egoism. But man, aware of the pointless nature of egoistic suffering, is not yet conscious of the meaning of his behaviour, the fact that everything he does has a second significance – that while he is preserving and saving the dimming flame of life within himself, on that other, historical scale, his will to self-preservation is serving the vast complex whole of a country at war.

Paralysis

(Confessions of a survivor of dystrophy)

This psychological episode has been reconstructed by me (in the first person*) on the basis of siege experience, as reflected in the stories of the people who lived through it.

I was sitting at my former working desk, having moved my chair close up against it, tightly pressed between the chair and the edge of the table – in a state of paralysis. I had been commissioned to do an important translation. That impulse was sufficient for my pen to move across the paper. But I was already thinking with revulsion that I would have to dip the pen and turn the paper over. If I had to reach for the edge of the desk and get the razor blade to sharpen the pencil, I carried on writing with a blunt pencil, or a pencil instead of a pen, so as not to have to reach for the pen. It wasn't a matter of lassitude or exhaustion, which by now were actually passing off. I had been running in circles for months. Spring had brought something of a pause; more precisely, a slowing of the tempo. And this slowing down

* In the blockade-era version (drafted no later than 1943), this account was written in the third person; Ginzburg made the shift to the first person in the 1960s.

revealed a malaise of physical indolence – a peculiar kind of retardation of the will.

The easiest activities to perform were the inexorable demands of the moment or those stemming from the inertia of familiar situations. It was psychologically easier, more feasible, to go off to the other end of the city to have lunch or drag a bucket of water up the stairs than reach out for a pencil sharpener. We were drawn along the roads to lunch by the powerful stimuli of procurement; the buckets, chopping the firewood were seen to by inertia and needed no intervention from the will. Every object which was not a part of the day's arrangements demanded a new relationship each time between itself and the will acting upon it. And each time it was agony. The will shrank and froze in fear at contact, at the slightest effort at acting upon a world which had become a source of perpetual suffering.

I didn't reply to letters from unoccupied Russia – for all sorts of psychological reasons, but mainly because there would be the fuss about an envelope (there were none on sale), buying a stamp and the post box. They were all the most trivial of actions but they weren't mechanical, not worn smooth by inertia, and so required willpower.

Hopeless activity aimed at satisfying incessant and monotonously recurring needs was automatic. It was sometimes hard to get started on these, harder than to carry them out for all their physical difficulty. So that before braving all the obstacles of a hostile world to get lunch, you had in addition, for example, to wash the tins out (you'd brought something home in them), wipe them with frozen fingers, swollen from the water. Again? Disgust! I can't! . . . But the effort to get started has been made. Revulsion subsides and now I even try to wipe the tins neatly round the rim with my fingers.

Indolence was a malaise of the will attended by symptoms of disgust and fear at contact with the world.

And the world will turn its other side . . .*

It turned the side of suffering towards us. At the end of the winter of '42, by no means everything had yet been real suffering, but the mind had been bruised by the expectation of suffering, by a still unconquered habituation to it.

War was the basic content of that world, its total reality. The factual and psychological totality of that war did not allow the scope for evading it that previous wars had . . . Everyone not directly involved knew (whatever the arguments) that he was cut off from common reality. He could of course consider his own life as more important than historical reality but he knew that the choice had been made.

Dystrophy was the extreme degree of this separation and even freed one from choice. It freed one from moral unease because we, the dystrophic realized that we had been sacrificed to the war, but what we didn't realize at that time was that we were also the community, in however dim and reflected a fashion. That the enemy wanted to kill me and I was alive, that he wanted to kill the city, but the city lived on and I was an almost unconscious particle of its resistant life.

That was something we did not know. Dystrophy gave a person a protective indifference, under cover of which he could die easy. It left a person face to face with the naked primordial ambivalence of satisfaction and suffering.

Winter is shining beauty, easy breathing and gay fire, soft snow, soft fur . . . But unvanquished winter is blackness, buckets that are frozen and heavy as stone; it is cold, always heart-achingly cold. The ways of conquering the world of things – conquerable by love, knowledge, construction – vanished in the chaos and collapse of the objects of civilization.

* This is a line from Nikolai Oleinikov's ballad, "Gluttony" (*Chrevougodie*) from 1932.

But after all, I was a dystrophic who survived and the ability to think had returned to me. I mentally allocated the phenomena of the world according to my judgment. But I agonizingly didn't want any physical contact with it. Everything was a painful irritation of the skin or mind. The great sufferings of winter had gradually been replaced by a constant nervous irritation.

I didn't always use my long-seeing spectacles. When I did put them on I loved the festive gaiety of the transformation. The world suddenly came closer and flared into life; I could also extinguish this brightness again when it hindered my concentration. But one day in spring – the trams had just started running – my glasses got broken on a tram (I'd put them in my pocket). I had the prescription but it turned out that one couldn't order the glass. There weren't any lenses. And the world was wiped out, extinguished. I would walk past the memorable Leningrad ensembles and could not return to them that slightly artificial iridescent definition I had so loved in the former life. That irritated me. This irritation dominated me so much that now I didn't want my visual integrity back at all.

It was even more agonizing with footwear. My galoshes were ripped. In spring, for example, it was wet feet for the most part, always wet feet. When you eventually reach your destination and sit down, you feel as if you had no socks or shoes on; your feet seem encased in heavy swollen rubber. My shoes (you couldn't get new ones) were warped and stiff as boards as well as having developed great lumps. I walked around with my head drooping, thinking about my feet. It was my feet which effected direct contact with the world. A repulsive contact.

I found out what it meant to limp on both feet – it's when neither foot can stand the weight of the body. Once, back in the former life I had enjoyed thinking as I walked. I had enjoyed that twin reciprocal rhythm of outward and inner

101

movement. I liked to hear my own breathing as I passed through the world on its streets and roads. Along our roads with their beautiful repetitions, prompting a blind desire to go on and on . . . with the perpetual illusory expectation of what would be finally revealed round the corner . . . With a certain inexplicable, illogical contempt for myself I recalled this now, as I slowly hobbled along.

Irritations and humiliations pervaded existence. At some canteens and offices there were lavatories, terrible, without water. There would be a queue to use them. People didn't hide the fact that they couldn't wait (one of the symptoms of dystrophy). In the editorial office where I used to go, there was only one lavatory.

The girls, ordinary girls usually without any indecent intentions, used to shout out to any man who had been sat there for any length of time for him to hurry up. The man (young) would reply coolly from behind the door – also without intentional indecency: "You want me to come out without any pants on, do you?"

Eating was also hedged round with a multitude of annoying conventions. During the time of the great hunger, the impulses propelling one towards eating used to override all the irritations. Now it was different. It started with buying things. It was always dark and damp inside the shop. Your feet were wet through and aching. And I was a disaster at coping with all the things you had to hold in your hands. With envious amazement I watched women manage their handbags and satchels with deft ease. I couldn't do that. I had to pull out my wallet, then my card after finding it in the wallet (without shaking out the others tucked in there with it). Then the money. There was pushing from behind and I couldn't get the change back in. Holding the change, the ration card and my wallet, I would go over to the counter, the briefcase clamped under my elbow slipping inexorably down. I was certain that my gloves would immediately be stolen if I stuck them in

102

my pocket. But if I didn't do so, then I certainly wouldn't have a single hand to deal with my string bag and the 300 grams of herring I hoped to put in it. Everything accumulated in my hands in the end – briefcase, wallet, string bag, change, gloves, the card, which I held onto for dear life – and the herrings, badly wrapped up by the assistant. I disgustedly crammed all this into a bundle and hugged it to me, as I hobbled over into the corner to an empty counter, to drop it all and sort it out – looking over my shoulder meanwhile to see that no one was sneaking up behind me.

The hostile world bore down on my body – that sore, toil-worn surface. And the body was the advance-post of this world, pressing down on the mind. Apart from anything else, guns fired in this world. Oddly enough, this was now perceived not as it actually was, a deadly danger, so much as an extra accompanying irritation. More harassment . . . No getting your lunch in peace. I'm not standing under the gateway with wet feet and a string-bag full of stuff. To hell with them! . . .

The world bore down on the sore, toil-worn mind. The best thing was for it to stay in a torpor. When it was warm in the room it wasn't a burdensome torpor. But beyond the windows in strange physical nearness, though measurelessly distant intellectually, lay the world, with its multitude of once-loved objects. Very close beyond the blank windows lay the city, the tormented city, which I should have found it hard to abandon even now. Harder than doing without the people who had left the city. I loved the city with all its celebrated symbolism, its fog and sleet, its smoke-reek and wind. Especially that wind . . . I knew how I could love my city – the empty streets, snowdrifts in the squares, the stricken houses . . . But now I was an aching surface and I was asking the city not to touch me.

I was accustomed to coping without the outside world. When it penetrated my consciousness that the sky was getting bluer, i.e. that buds and leaves would be coming, rustling in

the wind, I took fright, I feared the new season, bringing with it a threat to my torpor. I had a madman's fear that all this would be coming to an end. After all, that would mean the end of the life I was now leading, a strange, simple existence, stripped to the bare minimum, with its agony and intense relief. A complex difficult process of restoring normal or apparently normal life was going to begin, with all its tedious desires. But for the moment it was paralysis. The world, dimmed because of my broken glasses, impassable because of my warped footwear. A world without love. I sat in quiet torpor and any kind of love, past or future seemed to me an excessively bothersome business.

I was stricken with a peculiar siege malaise of the will. And the only longed-for, feasible way out was into an ordinary, human illness, like in the old days. It was impossible to be ill for a multitude of technical reasons. But illness, ordinary illness, would have been the ideal state. Dozy, clouded by heat, the mind would have put off all responses to the demands of a hostile world. Illness was the supreme right to paralysis.

The illness did come at last and the insurmountable everyday obstacles sorted themselves out in a totally unforeseen manner. Then I started to succumb eagerly to the malady; and it seemed I would never tire of it. Above all, man cannot bear an absence of goals. The illness, however, conferred a strange, and in its own way, unique combination of torpor with a constant purpose which seemed to be constantly achieved. Fever made necessary a weakened immobility, a detachment from a fearful world. It was a necessity, directly, physically felt, and its fulfilment was in itself purposeful. Thus the condition of fever, heavy dozing (dozing brings a special pleasure because it is a tangible, aware kind of sleep) was at the same time the recognition of a feasible necessary kind of negative action.

I lay there and all the miles I had traversed with my toil-worn feet receded, all the distances separating me from water, firewood, bread. I lay enjoying and took pleasure in

pushing torpor to its limits. Through immobility I gradually achieved the disappearance of the body. The loathsome, hostile, suffering body gave no further sign of its presence. A swimmer experiences something of the kind, when he lies on the water, eyes closed, without feeling it and the only sense left to him is that of his own deep breathing.

The sensation of breathing remained with me too. In my doze I kept track for a long time of how my breath, born in the depths, expanded and streamed upwards, as if it existed independently and was making its own way through an intangible body.

The heart got in the way of this blissful total alienation of the body. From the left side came occasional uncomfortable dragging sensations. I tried to lay my left shoulder and arm especially flat and immobile. To settle the heart. But the heart had to work. It was disagreeable to think that the heart must not stop for a moment, that it kept on and on at its self-devouring labour. And how long could it go on? . . . But the heart didn't always make itself felt.

So I was rocked on the waves of illness. And without thinking about it, I knew that this was the way people went into the easy death of dystrophy. Death without resistance. Death without surprise: there was a man and now he is no longer. Incredible! No, only too believable. The most likely outcome of all.

Death leaving no trace of life. The cat licks the plate clean.

Traceless all and so easy not to be . . .*

Not at all like Ivan Ilich. Not like Lev Nikolaevich Tolstoy.

But life was already beginning to shine through, with its surviving desires – the desire to live and the readiness to risk death – glimmering through the topor.

* This line comes from Fyodor Tyutchev's 1870 poem "Brother, who accompanied me for so long" (*Brat, stol'ko let soputstvovavshii mne*).

Excerpts from a Siege Day*

I

Urgency

N did not immediately understand why every day at work, around two o'clock, he was possessed by a strange sense of malaise. Then he realized what it was – urgency. This urgency was one of the guises of starvation or starvation trauma. Urgency as a mask for hunger – the ceaseless rush from one stage of eating to the next, accompanied by the fear of missing something. This urgency was particularly associated with lunch. This was given out by an indifferent government agency. That is, it had objective criteria for everything – the criteria certainly existed and they were certainly objective. But what if, suddenly, there wasn't enough? Several times during the winter there hadn't been enough porridge.

Nowadays canteens always give out everything they're supposed to. Nowadays urgency is a reflection of the mind, a race from one aimless goal to another. These goals are set in a circle, a repetitive series leading nowhere.

* These fragments originally formed part of the single "day in the life" of the hero, in the blockade-era manuscript "Otter's Day", and therefore connect with the first part of *Notes from the Blockade*.

If the motivation were just the usual ordinary feeling of hunger, it would be something heartening, reassuring. It is at precisely that time of day that it begins to sharpen. But the traumatized person can't stand feeling hungry; that in turn gives rise to lassitude and fear. N concentrates now on the desire to go out (his working day has not been standardized). He reads his typing, moving effortfully from line to line. The most unpleasant thing is transferring a correction from one copy to a second, then a third. A triple brake on his race. Nowadays he has to observe the decencies and he does so, meticulously slowing down his gestures. He speaks carelessly: "You give it in, then. I've got to go out just now. I'll be back before four, if anyone needs to know . . ."

Somebody enquires: "You off to the canteen?"

"Yes, that is I will be. I have some things to do first."

You can't reveal your hurry.

The secretary says in a bright voice: "You know it would be so nice if you signed this paper right now."

From her point of view it just means a delay of a minute or two. Sweet girl, she doesn't realize that she has cut into the internal headlong dash of a traumatized man and that it's painful.

By now N is unable to carry out a single braking movement. He can't get to his desk. He asks the secretary for a sheet of paper, although he has paper in his briefcase; it would mean snapping the lock of the briefcase again. He grabs the nearest pen, which barely works, sits himself down somewhere, and writes a few lines in an alien hand, gaining a minute that way. He writes thinking that he still has to overcome the exit to the street, the tram, the queue at the control point, the canteen queue, the deliberateness of the serving-girl . . . And in that series of problematic actions, the thing for the sake of which they are being carried out – a portion of soup and 200 grams of porridge – seems imperceptibly brief and ephemeral.

After the tram, there remains an extremely unpleasant stretch on foot. On the way he encounters people coming back from the canteen. It's hard to resist the question: "What is it today?" and you want to resist so as to keep all possibilities open. You can also make deductions from the way they hold their bags, lunch pails or briefcases. Round the corner he sights the entrance, always half-open. Now nothing (including air raids or shelling) will stop you going up to it and going inside. In the depths of the dark corridor there is a patch of light where the bald head of the server flickers by – the joyous sign of extra helpings. Sometimes though, the smooth surface of the counter gleams dismally.

During the winter (especially before the general evacuation) an hours-long queue used to stand here by the control point. They stood submissively. It seemed natural to employ every effort to get the lunch which saved them from starvation. Besides, people stood in a chilly corridor, not out in the freezing cold. Nowadays it was empty here – the reason being that everybody was in so much of a hurry. Getting their cards, money and passes mixed up, everybody wanted to push through the dam of the three or four slowly advancing backs; everybody had to get their tallies as soon as might be just to calm down (so long as the serving-girl hadn't lost them . . .) the old trauma was still working.

Nowadays this would seem to be an apparently third-rate canteen (an imitation of normal existence) with its un-watered flowerpots on the tables, half-grimy tablecloths, almost clean serving-girls. It may not be seen at once (during the winter everything was seen at once), that people here are acting out a tragedy. You realize this if you look closely; how they lick their spoons quickly (it isn't done to lick your plate any more), scrape their plates clean, tilting it up, running the finger round the rim of the tin of porridge, how they stop talking as the food is served and study it carefully, how their heads automatically turn to follow the serving-girl.

108

Of all the meals, lunch bore the least resemblance to its name. The soup still gives ground for hope. It's not very tasty and there's more of it; and after all, it is the first course. At lunch the saddest thing is eating the porridge; the briefest of acts, so brief that the start touches the finish. Two swings of the spoon are enough to wreak irreparable damage on the round fluffy mass doled out on your plate, with the dimple in the middle, and 10 grams of dark-golden oil poured over it.

II

After Lunch

Gloom over the empty plate, greasy from the porridge, signals the end of the pre-lunch rush. Here begins the lull of the siege day. There is nothing unprecedented in the phenomenon of the post-lunch lull. A real midday meal (not what a man grabs during his lunch break) was always a turning point. Late dinner at seven o'clock was always the direct transition to an evening's relaxation. The earlier lunches cut across the day. Chekhov affirmed that it was only possible to work before lunch. Lunch brings with it not only indolence and drowsiness, but also a sense of the onset of decrepitude, old age, exhaustion, the dying of the day. For many, these were the empty hours dragging on somehow, until the evening eventually took shape with its own conventions and goals.

Now that people were in primitive dependence on the length of the day, the temperature and the light – the feeling of the dying day was especially concrete. In the middle of the white nights – there existed this winter trauma, terribly tenacious, like all traumas that winter. In the post-lunch depression the sense of over-satiety was now replaced by disappointment, and an exasperation brought on by the swiftness of lunch.

The siege circle consists of repeated renewed segments. Post-lunch depression occurs with the same regularity as

everything else, the shelling for instance. The mind is not allowed the liberty to be depressed for long, and suddenly everything, which at other times is shrouded in mist, comes crowding in. The pointlessness of goals dawns with poignant pain, especially the repetition of the gestures accompanying the relentless race. And especially the feeling of being cut off. Cut off from those who have left the city for unoccupied Russia. They are unpicturable, their existence is unreal. Cut off from those running alongside . . .

N slowly walks back from the canteen to the office. On his right is the Neva at the far end of a side street. At the hour of depression one had to walk round that, not touch it. This summer it is only when his tram crosses bridges that he sees the mighty Neva with its warships. He never once touched the granite warmed by the sun with his hand, never sat on the semicircular benches, never descended the steps down to the water, unexpectedly intimate, palpable – with sand on the bottom and the smell of fish, suddenly revealed amid the decorative riverine view.

The corner of Fontanka* with an old house. Here N used to go visiting. The people he visited had been evacuated. He always used to arrive very late, getting ready to come much later than people went to bed nowadays. There was always vodka and light refreshments there. Strange . . . People sat and talked and talked. Read things to one another. Casually enquired: "Shall we have tea now or finish the reading?" "Finish, of course . . ."

Visiting friends, with supper delayed by conversations. Or this wind and the constant rush of foliage along the branches – that was all part of the former life. But depression has another card to play. It doesn't want it to return. Either because that other life is quite other, utterly

* One of the great waterways which run through central Leningrad (St Petersburg) in concentric semicircles.

inconceivable, or because there is too much resemblance – like a mirage.

Engrossed in his own thoughts, N walks on from the canteen to his office without looking about him. Suddenly a familiar, heavy, shuddering sound penetrates his consciousness. He realizes at once that this is not the first such sound, there have been several, one after another. A bombardment; in another district for the moment, apparently. Now N looks about him. If it hadn't been for the noise, you wouldn't have guessed what was going on. Passers-by went about their business with the Leningrad sang-froid which had begun to dominate normal behaviour completely. They walk along the street (until driven into an entrance) carrying their briefcases, lunch pails and string bags, stand in queues, chat and light up one another's cigarettes. You hear the repartee, "I think they're our guns". "Get away – ours!" Or: "That was a bang and a half!"

The repetitive noise doesn't leave his mind now. And as always when he hears that sound N experiences a mad sensation of things being overturned, turned inside out. Confusion in the categories of space and time. The whistle of the shells overhead is more frightening but more comprehensible. It indicates a spatial presence – they are really here over your head at this moment – and temporal extension (the duration of the whistling). The noise of the distant explosion is something else altogether. What was the untrackable present had already become the past by the time it reached the consciousness. The reverse order: first the sound, then the fear at what had not by now happened. Then the silence and in that brief silence, the question of the life and death of a person is decided. It is decided by the fact that he has taken two extra steps towards the tram stop, or bent down to retrieve a dropped briefcase or stepped off the pavement into the roadway. A person thinks everything will happen in order – there'll be a whistling, then an explosion which he'll see from

111

the side, then something will happen to him. He knows that's an aberration.

This is an aberration of the link between cause and effect, but there is also the aberration of security – when a person speeds up his step under bombardment, so it doesn't catch up with him. That is exactly what N does when he's annoyed at being stopped in the street and prevented from reaching the office, where there's a brew-up at this time and he could have a cup of boiled water to go with the sweet he'd got left over from lunch.

The emotion of fear is supplanted by one even more direct – exasperation, caused by hunger trauma. If this exchange of emotions did not take place, N would go into the entrance saying to himself and the others that one ought to behave sensibly – no panic and no silly carelessness.

III

Evening

The afternoon working hours were over. There remained the walk back home. In the first daylight exit from the office a nervous tension had prevailed; in the second it was torpor.

N slowly walks along the street. Now it is evening, before the onset of the white night, with a magnificent cold slanting light (even on muggy days), in which the asphalt of Nevsky Prospect glows. The usual astonishment when, after working late, you emerge from darkened rooms to find the light outside in undiminished brilliance. It is this inexhaustibility of ongoing life which real Leningraders love so much. It is a feeling of untouched reserves of life, waiting to be released each day.

Was it not from this that N had derived the dream which had occupied him when young? A dream of life made up of long days. Of days lived through and savoured in all their

112

protracted length and in every particle of their being. But nowadays the flow of life had its own laws – the white nights notwithstanding. The circle had to close (in order to begin again – hence the circle). The flow of existence is determined by weariness, the exhaustion of the ritual gestures of the day, the imminence of the last meal-time. The circle drearily seeks its non-existent end.

There is something disorienting in the non-coincidence of the state of the day and the state of the person. The undimming light tautens the nerves and serves as a reminder that it would be possible now to take a long walk along the winding river, and do a lot more besides . . . The night's cruelty is revealed during the white nights. Blok understood that: "May is cruel with its white nights . . ." They are cruel to the person who wants to be protected by the darkness, that wants to sleep like the dead. The day is filled with a multitude of distracting, confusing things which darken the mind. At night however, freed from fuss and clutter and unsoftened by the dark, the fundamental features of life stand out. It is more fearful now than it has ever been.

There is supposed to be supper at home, the final meal, the measuring point of the evening. In the former existence, the evening used to start late for N, drag on and on, turning into a nocturnal vigil until two or three or later. It was part of the day, quite often a working day, but essentially one permitting idleness; the only part of the day when idleness was easy and allowed. And everything around filled it with amusement, love, friendly conversations over vodka. It could all be looked forward to like a sort of relaxation. Especially when the relaxation was uninterrupted, and crossed into the next unit of time. When for example one didn't have to separate until next day.

Nowadays the surrogate for all that was supper. Consciously or unconsciously, an inadequate supper, boiled beet tops for example, without bread, gave an emotional colouring to the

113

afternoon. A proper supper on the other hand reconciled one like a happy ending.

Supper was over. N sits by the stove. There are shavings still burning out in it and the stove is giving off some smoke. With a long splinter, N stirs the brands in the confined metal space and lights up. In the former existence, the papirosa had its own typology. There was the papirosa before bed, and the morning papirosa, then the lazy after-lunch papirosa, one for business conversations, one for friendly chat. There were also papirosi which he finished off, with a squashed end and traces of lipstick.

During the siege months, the papirosa took on a multitude of new and important meanings. It became a way of physically suppressing hunger and deflecting one's thoughts from hunger. In an existence totally undesigned for pleasure, smoking a papirosa was virtually the only act of pure enjoyment unconnected with practical usefulness (like eating and sleeping were), rather the contrary. In its disinterestedly hedonistic nature, the papirosa was a kind of remnant of ordinary human life. The papirosa – especially the home-rolled type with the elaborate ritual of its preparation – was a reserve means of filling the vacuum, or some part of the emptiness. What else was there to look forward to? . . . What else was in store? . . . One could still have a smoke, one would reply to oneself, assuaging one's misery.

The papirosi varied during the course of the day. The hungry papirosa which N smoked just before his soup, when the serving-girl was going slow and irritation rising to a snapping point. The after-lunch papirosa had once appeared in a haze of intoxicating satiety; now it suppressed the miserable unsatisfying meal. The working papirosa. He enjoyed thinking about that on his way to the office. It was part of a communications complex with indifferent people, gossip, bureaucratic rituals and electric gadgets (economizing on matches there,

114

they lit their cigarettes on hotplates). There was also the final, evening papirosa. With its smoke, the mind, exhausted during the day, seemed to spend itself. Despite this thematic allotment of papirosi, smoking was all the same in that existence, perhaps the freest act, the least attached to any given situation.

N digs about in an oven niche with a long splinter, finishing the evening hand-rolled papirosa, which had carried on and extended the process of eating. The last glow, shrouded in ash, glimmered at the rim of the holder. And at that moment (it had happened more than once) the feeling of the circle, the race around the circle, suddenly seemed frighteningly clear. And most terrifying of all was not so much the repetition as the absolutely precise predictability. He sees the series of movements developing now, and those of tomorrow and the day after . . . He sees exactly how he picks up his briefcase, drops his key in his pocket, how he gets out of breath slightly as he climbs the office stairs, how he glances over the typist's shoulder – to see if the manuscript has got any further. Nothing can be subtracted from the linked series and nothing can be introduced which is not a predetermined, ritualized gesture.

All this is hardly new. The predictability of his future actions used to bother him in the previous existence too. He used to detach himself from his self and his double went forward into the future, automatically exact. For some reason it was particularly unpleasant when he was leaving town for a month or two. It was eerie to see in advance this alienated double getting his ticket, sitting in a carriage, opening a closed flat.

At that time they were mental mirages; in siege existence everything took on a strange literalness. Along with the gestures, the associated sensations were also predetermined. A feeling of confidence was bound to occur without fail at the moment when N proffered his pass to the guard outside

the office; a feeling of relief, when the right tram appeared from round the bend; a feeling of miserable emptiness when, under the first two blows of the spoon, the porridge vanished beyond recall; a feeling of fullness, inexhaustibility, when he took out the untouched bread from his briefcase in the morning.

Absolute unfreedom of mental activity, riveted firmly to things which had once stood on the very lowest rungs of the hierarchy of values.

In the urgent race from meal to meal, there was something unconscious, the polar opposite of those long days, utterly absorbed and digested by the mind, that had once been his dream.

Today, for some reason, there is a clarity of thought not experienced for a long time, a ferment of ideas seemingly intent on breaking free. Why had he remembered those long days? It means that the dystrophic blackout is starting to lift, the bond with communal life slowly strengthening, as that life stands firm against the enemy.

Draft "Theoretical Section" of the manuscript "Otter's Day" (excerpts)

Introductory note

The experience of the war inspired Lydia Ginzburg to draw profound historical and philosophical conclusions, which she eventually included in "Notes during the Siege", the opening section of "Around *Notes from the Blockade*". She elaborates on two insights that her generation, which suffered through two world wars and an intervening period of terror, had firmly grasped: "the ineradicability of social evil and the illusory nature of the individual consciousness." She reflects on the lessons of history in a comparative framework (in the context of Existentialism, for example) and with the benefit of hindsight (post-war Stalinism and renewed purges, which proved yet again the "ineradicability of social evil").

Even before the war had ended, Ginzburg was drawing historical lessons from the blockade experience and describing what she saw as the "catastrophic denouement of the one-and-a-half-century-long epic of the individualistic consciousness". She drafted what amounts to a political philosophy, treating the relationship between the individual and the absolutist (totalitarian) state with reference to Hobbes's *Leviathan* (1651). (Hannah Arendt and, after her, Giorgio Agamben, have famously discussed the experience of totalitarian terror – based

117

mostly on Nazi rule – in similar terms.) As has recently been discussed by Irina Sandomirskaia, Ginzburg brings Hobbes's model a step further than previous Russian intellectuals such as Alexander Herzen had done. For her, the Leviathan is not just a body politic – it is a *biopolitical* monster, with complete physical (food rationing) and political (the secret services) control. If Hobbes's Leviathan prevented the "war of all against all", the new Leviathan, as Sandomirskaia notes, "expropriates this violence and applies it in its own name" (see Irina Sandomirskaia, *Blokada v slove* [Moscow: Novoe literaturnoe obozrenie, 2013] p. 255, and the surrounding discussion on pp. 241–64). The subjects or "wards" of the Soviet State are unfree and cannot even ideologize their unfreedom – they are mere slaves. What is left to them is to search for "a loophole involving the least evil" (see p. 86 of this volume in "Notes during the Siege"). During the war, Ginzburg's pessimistic philosophy is brightened slightly by the example of Leningraders who are forming a heroic collective identity: perhaps, she hopes, there will be a rising sense of "citizenship", of communal values. But after the war, the state enters a "new debauch of social evil" (see p. 85 of this volume) and the hope dissolves. Thankfully, Ginzburg's belief in the word, in literature (which is a communal value), endures.

The pages below represent fragments of an archival draft for what became part of "Notes during the Siege." Their precise order could not be established: thus, an asterisk is used to mark the division between each fragment. These pages, drafted between 1943–5, were published in Russian, together with others, in *Passing Characters. Prose from the War Years. Notes of a Blockade Person,* edited by Emily Van Buskirk and Andrei Zorin (Moscow: Novizdat, 2011), pp. 292–8. Not translated here is the section on the psychology of the fear of death, because of its greater resemblance to the final version.

Certain of the ideas are expressed here only elliptically, in outline form. At times, clarifying words or phrases are

supplied in square brackets. The reader will find additional guidance in "Notes during the Siege" – for example, to notice that Ginzburg's comparison of night-time fear of bombardment in the blockade and the trepidation of earlier times makes oblique reference to the terror of 1937–8 (where "hit" refers to random arrests by the secret police). Those looking for a broader discussion of the "three paths" discussed in section one (those who initially opposed the revolution, supported it, or wished to be "fellow-travelers") may wish to read her expansive treatment of these choices, their causes and fates in her famous essays, "Generation at a Turning Point" and "At One with the Legal Order" (in English translation by Emily Van Buskirk and Alyson Tapp in *Lydia Ginzburg's Alternative Literary Identities*, edited by Emily Van Buskirk and Andrei Zorin [Oxford: Peter Lang, 2012], 369–99).

Draft "Theoretical Section" of "Otter's Day" (excerpts)

I

The system presented, in sharp relief, a historical problem that had already ripened: the transformation of the subjective person and [with it] the formation of a civic-minded person.

A government, which demanded of people that they – at every single point – wanted exactly the same thing as it wanted (bourgeois governments fundamentally do not require this).

The government demanded this in the most extreme and crude form.

It became difficult immediately after the transition was complete – from the enthusiasm of the revolution and the barricade to life's ordinary business.

It was difficult for all (thinking) people, because they were all heirs to the 19th-century consciousness.

Preconditions for a conflict with society. Three paths:

[1] Those who wanted something else (the counter-revolution).
[2] Those who wanted the fundamental aspect [of the revolution], and assumed responsibility for everything (the party intelligentsia) – their emptiness, the loss or risk of loss of established connections with society.
[3] Those who wanted the fundamental aspect [of the revolution] but did not assume responsibility for everything. They wanted to be specialists who would lay at the feet [of the revolution/party] feelings that were wise and expressed according to their own method. (The difference between those working in the humanities and in other spheres. To work in the humanities is [itself] the expression of wills.)

Their offer was not accepted. Collapse of work and creativity. A social emptiness too, since they had thought of their work and creativity as a way to participate in the culture of the country, of the collective.

Hence Otter's complex – a world that summons you nowhere, silence, indifference, laziness, etc.

The conflict took place not because the foundations were negated, but because of the extreme scope of the government's demands.

The historical meaning of this scope (for all the coarseness of its expression) is in the fact that the process of organizing uniformity of will was unusually new and difficult.

In the fact that the government was preparing for war while the general will was being realized.

In contrast, freedom of opinion and freedom of speech in the West did not justify itself, because it did not create a grand culture. It turned out to be the freedom to whine.

Whereas the governmental apparatuses of Western parliaments did not prove their ability to win the war.

120

II

History has devoted an interval of time to proving the impossibility and horror of an egoistic sense of life. With every means at its disposal it has reiterated and hammered home that the singular person has no value. It has repeated again and again – woe to the egoists and the hedonists: there is nothing in the world more defenseless and fragile than egoists and hedonists.

Open and masked forms of history's lessons. Under the masked forms people made use of many benefits and escaped many calamities – for a time. But they received the most terrible in full. Even more than their share, because they were decidedly unprepared for it.

A second ordeal cannot elicit a reaction that is like the previous one. History had proven the futility of this reaction. For a normal thinking person it necessarily elicited the reaction of disgust at egoism, which had condemned a person to the greatest helplessness and misfortune. This ordeal had to generate longing for a severe civic sense of life, which accepts the fact of death and accepts the burden of life, understood as connectedness. In this way a new consciousness must be born, which creates a new culture. For in the area of the culture of philosophy and the humanities, the subjective consciousness of the twentieth century already long ago lost its ability to create anything fruitful.

Two great illusions have been destroyed – here, the illusion of humanistic socialism; there [in the West], the illusion of humanistic individualism.

*

Thus, only now has the historical fate of this phantom generation and the symbolism of its fate become comprehensible. The first ordeal elicits an extremely individualist-hedonistic

reaction; the second proves the unfoundedness of this reaction. The combination of both of these acts within the bounds of a single generation is important, because humanity comes to know the truth only on the basis of its own experience, never on the experience of other generations.

In order to prove to a generation the futility of humanism, its incapacity to solve the contemporary tasks of life and the tragic doom of egoism, it was necessary to completely turn a generation into mincemeat. And history made it into mincemeat. The generation turned out to be the experimental material of history. And history burned and disemboweled it and turned it into a bloody mess. The end results were inevitable; the only discussion could be about whether the forms were open or masked.

In its open form fascism turned people into slaves, condemned them to eternal burdens and deprivations in the name of the Leviathan's interests, subjected them to systematic extermination and systematic moral decay. It deprived them of human dignity, their very human likeness and placed them in front of the spectacle of their own baseness, decay and disgrace. And people understood. That is, for now certain people have understood, and the majority has inwardly matured to the point of understanding that egoism as the measure of human behaviour is similar to death, that hedonistic individualism and humanistic socialism are untenable; and this is on account of two factors that have been revealed emphatically – the illusory nature of individual existence and the ineradicability of social evil.

Those who were condemned to physical annihilation and moral decay lost, more easily than others, the illusion of the absolute value of the individual consciousness (soul). Perhaps at last they will realize that everything valuable in a person, the very idea of value belongs only to the basis of the community. Culture is a phenomenon of connection. The word is the condition of the spiritual life of a person – it is a factor of

association. The absolute value of a singular consciousness is an illusion, a psychological aberration of individualism.

The new method of examination corresponds to the new (at this point still predominantly negative) concept of a person. The psychological novel of the 19th century arose on the great illusions of individualism. Now the examination of a person as a closed, self-sufficient soul has a sterile, imitative quality. The contemporary understanding is this: not a person, but a situation. The intersection of biological and social coordinates, from which the behaviour of a given person is born, the way this person functions. A person as a function of this intersection. This dismal analytical method does not occur to me as valid for all times, but as the most adequate for the negative concept of a person that exists at the present moment.

The second discovery of an anti-hedonistic order is the discovery of the ineradicability of social evil. Together with the refutation of the value of the single individual it separates, to the highest degree, people of the 20th century from people of the 19th. The latter piously believed in the eliminability of social evil by social means – this was the very premise of humanistic socialism.

It turns out that social evil cannot be eradicated – only replaced. That is, in the place of the evil that has been eliminated, another one rises up quickly and dialectically (concrete examples include freedoms, the mutual displacement of higher and lower cultures, families, women, etc.). The question lies only in the historical dialectic of choosing the more suitable evils, the lesser evils.

It is not a matter of extirpating social evil, for this is impossible – it is a matter of finding a *relationship* to it. A relationship is a defense; otherwise evil collapses on the naked egoist like a crushing hammer. A salutary relationship (the acceptance of necessity) can be found only in ascetic citizenship.

*

In the conditions of open forms, a generation lost important motivating illusions of the 19th century; beyond that, it lost all possibilities of the kind of (creative) activity that takes initiative of one's own; lost the inertial forms of everyday life; lost even the substitutes for material goods.

But at one time they started to prime this generation for these substitutes, in order to furnish it with some kind of content for their lives. But the pre-war economy and politics could not sustain this. This had to be stopped short and replaced by the slogan of preparedness for mobilization. This was the last blow. The generation lost everything, including a human image and likeness.

In the interval this generation's position was horrible, worse than it could have even suspected. The second ordeal gave its existence a kind of historical meaning. The meaning was that of the terrible, catastrophic denouement of the one-and-a-half-century-long epic of the individualistic consciousness (there was no one to think about this. If there were people who could think, then they would have thought about this).

During the time of the greatest unfreedom the generation attained the semblance of inner freedom and independence through the awareness of the fact that the difference between open and masked forms [of evil] is unimportant. Does it make any difference whether such-and-such people didn't take advantage of certain rights and benefits, if the result was one and the same? And it even happened that the greater the rights and benefits – the worse the result (again there arises the problem of the replaceability of social evil).

Within the open form, the difference between winners and losers turned out to be even less significant. And the losers who were in the most unpleasant circumstances received satisfaction from this. Where are the careerists and the establishments where they were making their careers? Here stand their empty, looted apartments. And their owners toss about along the roads [of war]. What difference is there between

124

published and unpublished books, if there are neither authors nor readers? For people belonging to the generation doomed to extermination, the definition of success was not to die.

Thus people who had skipped over the offenses and calamities that had oppressed them quickly accommodated themselves to new ones.

*

In the relative stabilization of reality there is both strength and weakness. The difference between the East and West, generally speaking, is greatly exaggerated. But in regard to the present discussion, there is a difference. The West, with its masked forms and hedonistic illusions, turned out to be psychologically unprepared. The East, in contrast, for decades (and in the sense of historical tradition, from time immemorial) was raised in the spirit that [as the saying goes] "our planet is badly equipped for merriment". This sense worked out a great number of qualities that are useful in such circumstances as these – a relative indifference to life, patience, endurance, habituation to calamities, and the conviction that calamities are what make up the normal form of existence. All of these are the characteristics of armies of serfs, which, however, were cancelled out by another of its attributes – lack of initiative. These qualities, however, formed the basis of a sui generis (passive) heroism. Thus is the psychological essence of a [peasant? – incomplete word in the manuscript] heroism (anecdote about the person). People will withstand calamities, because nothing else remains for them to do. And at that people will withstand them rather calmly, because they are indifferent, capable of endurance, and accustomed to calamities.

But the weakness is in the fact that what has taken place is only a quantitative strengthening, an amplification. No new quality was born that would bring with it enthusiasm and new initiative. With its habituation to calamities the East

provided an average level of behaviour (the ability to stand firm), whereas not being habituated, the West provided either disintegration, collapse (France) or an upsurge (England). For the Englishman the circumstance where they send him to dig trenches or dispatch him up to the roof is exotic, a factor belonging to a dizzying, new, unrecognizable reality, for him these are completely new demands by the Motherland, which are therefore exciting. But . . . take a fascist person, for whom all of this is a still more unpleasant continuation of habitual compulsions – to which he reacts with the habitual attempt to evade them, and in the case of failure – with passive endurance. In contrast to the first case, this life material does not turn into an ideological value and, therefore, does not serve as a condition for realization – that says it all.

*

People want to realize themselves. And members of the intelligentsia in particular, with their craving for ideology, wanted to change. At first it seemed to them that everything had changed and that they would change, would purify themselves from filth. The initial relationship to work, the dedication of the executive officer. The appeal to Olga Berggol'ts (it is awkward to speak of money), Nata goes to the hospital, etc. etc. The attempt to overcome the customary compulsion with inner volunteerism and by this means to find a path towards realization and initiative. All of this runs up against a powerful machine that is completely unadapted for taking into account psychological motivations. With customary rudeness and distrust towards good will, the machine throws a person from some sectors and draws him forcibly into others. The collapse of the intelligentsia's illusions in relation to the soul-saving properties of physical labour (conversation with the experienced Maximovich, the first trenches, the tour). It turns out that it is cruelly difficult, endlessly dull,

126

ineffective. The line of the intelligentsia's evasion [of duty] prevails, for this is in accordance with social law.

What the Leviathan needs from the *intelligent* is exactly the same as before (on slightly different material) – service [one word illegible in the manuscript]. And it quickly and firmly returns them to this business, providing, as before, certain goods and indulgences. What's different is that desiring people now have certain inner motivations [stemming from] the temporary necessity (value) of this condition. But those who had avoided a cynical sense of life had always been able to find motivation.

And so, the result was a reality that very much resembled [the previous one], and in certain features – to a horrifying degree. In one feature especially. The details of the resemblance – waiting in the evenings; the fear of falling asleep. So as not to experience this horrible awakening, people preferred to stay awake, waiting through the most probable time; the expectation of a noise in tense silence; the morning's uncertainty about what happened at night; the gradual discovery; the chance hit, the ways of reassuring oneself by discussing how this hit was somehow justified, and therefore could be avoided; the supplying of motives.

The old arguments about which is worse – this or that. Worst of all turned out to be the combination of both. Their combination was unbearable. A layered psychological cake, mixing ours and theirs. The twofold function of ours, which darkened one's reason. The analogy that was not accidental – in both cases we have a social evil that acts openly (evil without a mask), a hostile world, emancipated from all the factors that had restrained it.

What they received was an unchanged and monstrously hyperbolized reality. The principle is the same. The Leviathan uses to its advantage a person who internally does not meet it halfway and therefore is transformed into a slave, that is, into an organism that is deprived of common values and personal

initiative. All of this attained symbolic clarity and a hyperbolic extreme in the current conditions. Unfreedom penetrated into all of a person's manifestations, all the way up to the very minutest ones; meanwhile, this was outside of any kind of regulation, which itself legitimizes and ideologizes unfreedom. Passivity (lack of initiative) is hyperbolically underscored by the fact that everything happening presses on and crushes a person, but he himself does not participate in anything, until the Leviathan extends its tentacles in order to grab him and use him to its advantage. If in stagnant conditions he has not become needed by the Leviathan, then he is doomed to the kind of idleness that, probably, is how they punish sinners in Hell. He is in the midst of everything, everyone is next to him (the building blocks), he suffers everything, but he himself does not participate, does not do anything. He does not know or see this idleness, though it threatens him with annihilation at any moment. He is closed in his circle and runs along the circle, purposelessly repeating uniform movements next to others who are running along the same circles that do not intersect [with his]. (The ring [of the blockade], the circle, the day.)

The psychology of a slave, that is of a person who has no values, who does not even present himself to himself as a value, whom nothing touches and who is directed by desires that are straightforwardly egoistical, the urges closest at hand. In the given conditions this psychology also became manifest to a hyperbolic degree. A fashionable illness [dystrophy] brought it to a symbolic clarity. Its basic features are: a beastly clinging in the pursuit of the most petty egoistic goals, and the loss of feeling of all immaterial values, including one's own, which leads to indifference to life and death that is strangely combined with this petty clinging [to life] (the easy death of dystrophics).

The point is that tenacity is only stimulated by the unmediated impulses of suffering and pleasure – a return to an animal state.

128

Preface to "A Story of Pity and Cruelty"

"A Story of Pity and Cruelty" gives a raw and powerful account of the death of a close relative in the Leningrad Blockade, from the perspective of a survivor haunted by guilt and remorse, and recovering from starvation. The lives of two family members, whose mutual antagonism has long ago hardened into fixed patterns, hang in the balance; as they divide insufficient food rations on any given day, one morsel more or less for either person may determine the difference between life and death. The hero's guilt is not lessened, but rather made crudely material by the harsh conditions of the siege – he measures his guilt in words, in grams of bread.

This narrative, probably drafted in 1943 or 1944, was seemingly unknown even to Lydia Ginzburg's close friends. Not only did Ginzburg not publish it – it appears she never returned to revise it, in contrast to the large quantity of desk-drawer writings she actively prepared for press between her first opportunity to do so in 1982, the ensuing years of glasnost, and her death in 1990. The power of the text comes in part from its rawness and proximity to the experiences it describes. And yet even if it is unfinished, one could also say it is complete: for example, nearly identical passages at the beginning and end, where the hero receives a postcard from his brother, form a narrative circle that purposefully

leaves its hero in the state of remorse, despite his progress in post-traumatic self-analysis and understanding. The story was drafted (partly in pencil, partly in ink) in several small "school" notebooks without covers, which were tucked out of order into a dark red binding within a folder that contained another draft manuscript about remorse over the death of a father figure (more on this narrative below). An eleven-page remnant of an earlier version suggests that the text we have is a second draft. The story, left untitled by Ginzburg, was published in Russian as "A Story of Pity and Cruelty" ("Rasskaz o zhalosti i o zhestokosti" in *Passing Characters. Notes of a Blockade Person. Prose from the War Years*, edited by Emily Van Buskirk and Andrei Zorin (Moscow: Novoe izdatel'stvo, 2011). The editors chose the title based on a passage from *Notes from the Blockade* where Ginzburg gives a small sketch (from "Among the siege stories I have collected") of the tense relationship between two relatives, resembling Otter and Aunt (see p. 69 of this volume). "O" takes care of a much older sister when she is already "in an irreversible condition of dystrophy". Ginzburg writes that he "was irritated by her growing uselessness and the sacrifices he had made and continued to make for her sake. He told her of this with a roughness which astonished him. But immediately alongside this, there existed another layer of consciousness where it would be obvious that without his sister, the silence would be final and beyond belief." And she ends the passage with: "thus was the siege story of O, a story of pity and cruelty" (in the 1960s draft she had added, elusively: "but to this blockade story I shall still return").

"A Story of Pity and Cruelty" is a barely fictionalized account of the death of Ginzburg's mother, Raisa Ginzburg, who perished from starvation in Leningrad in November 1942. Readers will find reflections of the following basic biographical details in the text: Raisa Ginzburg was born Rakhil' Davidovna Gol'denberg in 1867 (making her seventy-five in

1942, Aunt's very age) and grew up in a relatively wealthy Jewish merchant family that came to financial ruin around the time of her marriage to Yakov Moiseevich Ginzburg. She never worked, and was supported by her husband (who died in December 1909), then by his brother, Mark Moiseevich (who died in 1934), and finally by her two children, Viktor and Lydia. Ginzburg's niece Natalia Sokolova (in a memoir tucked in her own archives in Moscow at RGALI) singled out "light-spiritedness" as her grandmother's signature quality, and observed that Raisa and her daughter had sharply divergent personalities. Ginzburg's brother Viktor (who went by the pen-name Tipot), a fairly successful dramaturge, moved to Moscow from Odessa around 1922, and by the time of the war had a daughter (Natalia Viktorovna) and two grandsons. As letters testify, he occasionally sent money to support his mother at his sister's request. Lydia Yakovlevna was her primary caregiver: from the early 1930s until her death, Raisa Ginzburg lived with her in a communal apartment at 24 Griboedov Canal in Leningrad.

Neither *Notes from the Blockade* nor "A Story of Pity and Cruelty" present themselves as autobiography, and yet the male heroes at the centre of both (a clear element of fiction) have a basis in Ginzburg's life experiences. Common to all of them is their work at the Leningrad Radio, aspirations to be a writer, membership in the Writers Union (which grants life-saving access to a second cafeteria in addition to that for radio workers), and apartment location in the centre of the city. Yet in *Notes*, whose events take place mostly in spring/summer 1942, N lives alone, whereas Otter in this story lives with his aunt. During this same period, Ginzburg lived with her mother, her sole dependant whose life she tried and failed to save. The almost complete omission of such a personally important, and traumatic, experience from *Notes from the Blockade* is striking, especially given the documentary aesthetic of Ginzburg's prose. (Details from "A Story

131

of Pity and Cruelty" surface in certain passages of *Notes*, such as the one about burnt cutlets and withheld candy, as well as in more generalized discussions about family relationships and in the emotional valence of food.) The relationship between Ginzburg's personal narrative about remorse and her more generalized historiographic piece evokes, in some ways, the example of Alexander Herzen, one of her most admired writers (along with Proust and Tolstoy), who omitted the story of his own family drama, and guilt, from the publications of *My Past and Thoughts*; it appeared only after his death (Ginzburg wrote about this in her book *On Psychological Prose*).

Two strange features of Ginzburg's text are particularly deserving of commentary. The first is the transposition of a mother–daughter relationship to that of an aunt–son in the process of fictionalization. This transposition occurs not only in "A Story of Pity and Cruelty", but also in earlier draft works that Ginzburg left unpublished – thus, it did not originate in the attempt to describe the death of a relative. She characteristically inscribed her autobiographical experiences into a male "other", sometimes symbolically named "Otter" – in this she followed Russian literary tradition, which presents male experiences as the most universal. Ginzburg also used this manner to write about lesbian love, inscribing her experiences into those of a male character. The decision to portray her mother as "aunt" no doubt has complex psychological origins (a rejection not only of the mother, but also of Freudian analysis), but there is another "family" logic. Since Ginzburg's uncle Mark Moiseevich took over family responsibilities after the death of her father, he was both uncle and stepfather – making her mother into an "aunt".

The second strange feature of "A Story of Pity and Cruelty" deserving special mention is the disorienting opening of the text, which confuses the perspectives of the two characters, Otter and Aunt, while making reference to an earlier death.

This death is one that Ginzburg had written about roughly a decade earlier (around 1934), in "Delusion of the Will" (published partially in 1988 and fully in 1989). Here, her autobiographical hero copes with his guilt over the death of his father – a quasi-fictional treatment of the death of Mark Moiseevich Ginzburg. Ginzburg seems to endow Aunt with an impossible perspective on her own death (which readers later learn was unconscious, and in any case was only "a death" from Otter's point of view), while also attributing Otter's remorse over both deaths to Aunt herself. The confusion of viewpoints may be a consequence of the difficulty of beginning the narrative.

"Delusion of the Will" contains philosophical reflections on the importance of remorse and guilt for art and memory. Through remorse and guilt, the twentieth-century consciousness that is otherwise disconnected, fragmentary, and isolated finds evidence of the reality of existence, the lasting significance of our actions, and the strength of the bonds that connect us. "A Story of Pity and Cruelty", which alludes to the other narrative in several places, is more story-driven and less directly philosophical. It probes the past with harsh honesty and analytical fervor, but it also abounds with circles and repetitions, which simulate confusion. Reading "A Story of Pity and Cruelty" alongside *Notes from the Blockade* and "Delusion of the Will", it becomes clear that this story connects to larger dilemmas of the twentieth-century person, and sheds light on questions of ethics and narrative involving a person whose very identity through time is in doubt. An individual traumatized by involvement in another person's death, through the act of self-analysis, is just beginning to recuperate an identity, in parallel with a new understanding of the humanity of the deceased. This new understanding is explicitly presented as conditioned by the death of the other, which suggests a frightening paradox: one can only understand certain experiences after one has

been released from them, in other words when one has ceased to be one's former self – regaining some humanity, perhaps. Because sympathy and clarity come later, on the other side of the experience and as a result of distance, there remains the question of whether true understanding of *that self* is possible. As Ginzburg observes in *Notes from the Blockade*, "The well-fed do not understand the hungry, themselves included."

Emily Van Buskirk, 2016

A Story of Pity
and Cruelty

She liked to say: "I've noticed that everything in my life is repeated twice."* (It was one of her generalizations.) And Aunt kept recalling this when she was dying. Because it was all very similar to the death of her husband. So for her it was like a bad dream when in the middle of it you realize you've had this dream before. It was similar in the very succession of symptoms. But it was especially similar in the way remorse and fear predominated, remorse more than any other feelings. And especially in the way the caring came too late, the way what was being done for her body when it was already insensible had been so much needed by that body when it was still alive. Because those very same burdens, which we think we can't possibly lift when we are looking ahead to infinite stability and repeatability, become inevitable and to be taken for granted when they are a unique final effort. It was similar, and at the same time it went immeasurably further in literality. The

* The death of aunt's husband was narrated by Lydia Ginzburg in her c.1934 story "Delusion of the Will" (in which the relationship between Aunt and old man is configured as that of brother and sister, rather than husband and wife). Coincidences between the circumstances of Aunt's own death and those of her husband's happen of course only once in the present story, though they are mentioned several times.

circumstances around the death of the old man, like those around many other calamities, had long surprised Otter* by their literality. Undisguised social evil gave reality to the metaphorical, metaphysical meanings connected with the set of words "poverty", "neglect" and "humiliation". But that was all left far behind when compared with the horrifying directness and literalness of the meanings which had to be lived through now. The formula "To share your piece of bread with your loved ones" turned out to mean: "Should you halve the bread you've received on both your worker's and your dependant's ration card, or keep an extra 100 or 200 grams of it for yourself?" It meant forcing yourself to pause and to cut in half that sweet made of oilseed husks.† And the saying about helpless parasitic old people consuming the life of a young man (with his worker's ration book) acquires a new etymology – he consumes, he eats, he eats up that which the other person himself could have eaten – as well as a completely new literality. What did people know about loneliness and neglect when they repeated the empty phrase "It's as if I'm living in a desert." What did they know of living without a telephone, living with the town's spaces monstrously separated one from another by thirty-five degrees of frost and the absence of trams. Of living when people who used to exist nearby are now – perhaps existing, perhaps dead – somewhere on Vasilievsky Island or on the Petrograd Side‡ beyond the frozen frontiers of the rivers. When you cannot possibly meet – you cannot possibly even want to meet (what would it be for?) – those who used to be your acquaintances. Later those people went away, one after the other. And when the

* The name is invented by Lydia Ginzburg and is apparently based on French "*L'autre*" and/or "*auteur*": the protagonist is her "other".
† Sweets made from husks of pressed oilseed, eaten as a delicacy during the blockade.
‡ Regions of Leningrad located across the Neva River from the centre.

frost ended and the trams started moving, there was no one left whom you could have dropped in on; and that very habit and need had been lost.

Empty apartments, with the locked – or, still worse, not locked – rooms of those who have died or been evacuated or are fighting at the front. A silence that roars in your head, silence that hinders your movement and makes it hard to breathe. That was what "It's as if I'm living in a desert" meant now.

Be content with the life you have.
Quieter than water, lower than grass –
Oh, children, if you only knew,
The cold and dark of the days to come*.

If you knew what coldness and darkness are, when they are not a metaphor. We who kept saying, like children, that every ordinary little thing grows into an unsolvable task – what did we know of *unsolvability* when it is not a metaphor? The lavatory has frozen. The drainage lids in the yard don't work. The House Manager forbids us to pour stuff into the rubbish pit: "You've frozen the drain, now warm it up any way you like."

As if that isn't enough – the bucket is leaking. Not by any exertions, nor by any means (not even for bread), can you find someone who will solder it together. All of this is altogether irremediable. The baths either don't work or else require longer hours of standing in queues than you have strength for. Indoors the cold is severe. There are no buckets. The task of washing cannot be solved. All you can do is live in a crazy torpor, letting these tasks pass you by. All the figurative meanings out of which our formulas for difficulties and privations were constructed have become absolutely literal.

* Last lines of "A Voice from the Chorus" by Aleksandr Blok (1880–1921), poem of 1910–14.

139

And this literalness weighed heavily on an old, helpless, weakening human being. He covers himself with rags, gets covered with lice, scarcely ever crawls out any more from a heap of ragged bedding (right here in his old room where they used to sit drinking tea in the evenings and chatting). Everything that torments his body, everything that heaps up around his body – is unsolvable. Better not to even touch all this, as the touching may only irritate him. Then at the moment when the insolubility reaches an extreme and desperate limit – the whole thing is solved by death.

This was very similar, but it went much further in simplification, outspokenness and literality. And guilt, too, the material of guilt, left all the past far behind itself. It almost stopped being psychological and with horrifying crudeness became embodied in words, in gestures and in the calculating of grams and slices.

And as guilt grew and increased, remorse accordingly lessened. Perhaps because the guilt was now too big to be felt to its full extent, or because a human being cannot go through the same inner experience twice, or simply because of fatigue.

But, whatever the reason, a conversation with himself about it all began straight away and continued: with pusillanimous digressions, with tricks and postponements, but it continued. And he knew he would have to talk it through to the end.

We are mistaken, by the way, when we unreservedly reproach people for sentimentalizing over their dead, after they have poisoned the lives of the living. It is not simply thoughtlessness, which the fact of death disperses; it is an instantaneous alteration of all impulses of behaviour and judgment. Impulses of irritation, of malice and of despair about the insolubility of all life's tasks fall away. Meanwhile other, positive, impulses, hitherto present in suppressed form, are set free and become active. We were doomed to such

cruel and constant suffering by the life of someone close to us that the first moment after that person's death has inevitably brought a sense of relief, a sense, above all, that everything unsolvable in that person's existence has been solved. This death, bringing liberation from intolerable burdens and sufferings, is just what was needed for one's consciousness to recover and to become able, after a certain interval of time, to apprehend the psychological horror of the death. Thus death has turned out to be the necessary condition for one to relate to death in a human way. More than anything it has turned out to be a prerequisite for the purely physical relief and calming of the organism, and even for a relative satiety, all of which merely made room for the hard emotional work of repentance and pain, and cleared a space for anguish.

In the first days everything hurt and nothing could bear to be touched. He was tormented by an ineradicable anguish which was worst in the crucial hours following a meal. Pieces of their life crowded his memory. Sometimes he picked through them, sometimes thrust them away in search of relief. But he knew that in the end he would have to put it all in order. He must put it in order, otherwise he would never cope with it. In reply to his telegram V had sent him a postcard which was not a good one. It had on it the phrases "our darling", "our beloved old lady", which had a depressing effect on Otter, both because he did not consider that either he or V had the right to utter such words and because these words, despite being unjustified, nonetheless chafed him like a reproach. There had in fact been no idyll. But the words "beloved old lady" were so horrifyingly unlike what had happened, so unlike everything he had done. If only they were just slightly true, a little bit true . . .

V wrote: "I must be to blame for something with regard to her, but I can't sort this out at the moment." How like V that was, with his good character. V sensed the pain and the guilt which every one of us inevitably feels when we hear of

the death of someone close to us. V was a wit, a very clever, well-qualified wit. But – a man of speech. In writing he lagged behind himself and was more provincial, showing a lack of culture. And he bluntly wrote the words which pain drives up from the depth of our consciousness but which nevertheless remain prohibited. For him everything would quickly pass and, of course, he would never sort any of it out, nor would he try to. To his younger brother, a man of bad character, he left not only all the burdens of care but also all the torments of remorse and self-blame.

He, however, really will sort it out . . .

There are several different aspects here, different lines. They are painfully mixed together. Perhaps it will be easier if they are disentangled. One is: pity for oneself. Another is: pity for her. There is pity for that unhappy life in the last months, and – yet another aspect – regret that she has died. And – separately – the detailed recollection of the process of death. And finally – the main thing – guilt and repentance. All this has to be analysed separately. Analysed in the strictest possible way, yet also, perhaps, in a mitigating way; and a balance has to be found. All the same – whatever it was, even if it was a great crime, even if murder – all the same his life and work will continue. That is a law of nature. It will happen in any case, indisputably. Therefore, instead of blindly driving needles under one's fingernails, it is better to think systematically . . .

First – pity for oneself. The problem of one's own loss. This seems, after all, the easiest to cope with. Yes, indeed, he is tormented without respite by an anguish that makes him helpless. Anguish that makes him keep wanting to change his position, because in every position he feels bad. At home, he feels it would be much easier at work; at work he straight away starts hysterically hurrying home, where you can lie down beneath a blanket. Whereas in fact it is too cold and too quiet at home. He recalls certain people, known to him

only slightly, who for some reason have not left. Hurriedly, sparing no effort, he seeks them out in the manic certainty that with them he'll immediately feel better. But these strangers become an unbearable load on his nerves which he must get rid of as quickly as possible. Not one of his failures, not one of his losses in love, which caused him great suffering, ever brought this unique nostalgic yearning. Only once in his life did he experience something like it when, scarcely out of adolescence, he left home for the first time and went off to an unfamiliar town. It was just after the Civil War, at a time of ruin, when spaces and communications were terribly hampered, and home seemed almost irretrievable. Then, too, for a long time – until he got used to it – he was oppressed by a helpless, objectless anguish.

The present anguish, too, was objectless. There was no purposefulness in it, no vain desire to bring back something that had gone. Indeed, one could not possibly want to bring back the unsolvable heaviness and darkness of the year that had passed. One could not want to bring back that terrible rotating wheel. But the sudden stop made him feel sick. His body couldn't immediately adapt to the removal of a burden which had become part of itself. He yearned, not for the human being, who for a long time had scarcely been there, but for the habits which had developed through suffering and had arranged themselves in the only possible form of existence; he yearned for those justifications of the cycle of movements which was renewed every day. Existence had lost the compulsory shape which made it possible; what lay ahead was to find a new shape – this required time. Meanwhile the lightness of it made him feel sick.

That was the top stratum of anguish. But beneath it lay deeper strata. With this death he had lost the last remnant of his youth. He had lost the permanent basis of everyday life – it had weighed him down and irritated him and yet it was the firm and abiding element of family life which survived love's

bonds and rifts and preserved a shape for day-to-day living. He had lost the last of the difficult, unavoidable human obligations, and thus the last of his humanity. Socially he had become lightweight to the point of weightlessness, now that everything had gone which gave weight to the words "head of the family". Indifference threatened to become absolute. So in the deeper strata the anguish was a yearning for his own humanness.

Sometimes, when it increased and was more intense, it brought with it a mad desire to go back. He wanted the sitting by the stove, the stupefying hassle about food, the body heavy from eating foraged cabbage (these were the best memories that passed through his mind), and the sated cigarette and Aunt's standard question: "Had a smoke yet? How I used to dislike it when you smoked. But now I've come to like it. When you smoke you are very nice."

It all seemed to him filled with lost human meanings. Even if poor and painful, it was a way of life in which everything cohered: slop-pail, oil-lamp, different-sized frying pans – each thing had its significance.

That way of life was a cycle of eternally renewed physical difficulties and hardships, yet it contained psychological possibilities – of having a rest, of shutting oneself off. The stirring of the saucepan, the stomach crammed with foraged food, the lazy cigarette, the stumbling, elusively aimless conversation with his aunt, even the squabbling and the irritation – it was all a kind of rest; for it all justified stopping his hard mental labour. An excuse for idleness.

And while he was tearing individual images out of their terrible context, he wanted them, longed for them. But then the terrible context would make itself clear and almost imperceptibly those images would be replaced by others borrowed from the past. His past life had shifted away and he didn't want the people who belonged in it. In his mind he would see himself sitting as a guest in the home of one or another of

144

them, and nearly every time there was a sense of its all being unnecessary and boring, even repulsive. That was not what he wanted. Better just take what was on the table and carry it off home. That was what he wanted. He wanted his aunt's little room (with the bourgeois pretensions that made him angry), he wanted the lamp to be lighted, he wanted someone who had dropped in by chance to be sitting there at the table or, best of all, their communal-apartment neighbours*, and he definitely wanted his aunt to be sitting there or, rather, to be moving around the room, made happy by the guests and the conversations (it annoyed him if she joined in too much). He wanted it all so much that he did not even bother to visualize what was actually on the table or how they ate it. This was what he wanted from his past life. The humanity. The awareness that he, head of the family, had provided a helpless creature with an easy and worthwhile life. People chattered, smoked, ate things from the table. Aunt poured out the tea. Aunt's life was of his making and at this moment it seemed to him successful (some other moments were quite different). It was good, it was right. Precisely *this* image of his past life now accompanied him and stirred up a longing. This was what he wanted. But of course it could never come back. And to want the other thing, to want the life recently experienced, was madness, derangement.

Now at last he tries to clarify the question of pity for oneself, the question of one's loss. Yes, he has lost the remnants of his youth and humanity, lost a way of life and a home. Yet everything he's been remembering – the cabbage stalks, the cigarette, the evening conversations – was from the "breathing-space" period.† What would have to be experienced in the winter could, essentially, *not* be experienced.

* Other families who shared one's apartment after the post-revolutionary division of large apartments into two or more small ones.
† See note to p. 8 of *Notes from the Blockade*.

145

It would be the utmost limit of all life's insoluble problems, a limit threatening a deathly outcome. Frozen buckets of sewage, water got from the cellar, unobtainable firewood, never-ending physical pains. Again the exhaustion* and inability to work, the body letting you down at every step. To pity yourself, to pity the loss of your humanity and of a certain way of life, is close to hypocrisy or horrid sentimentality. A spiritual luxury, to which his cruel existence gives him no right. And in general, once you start feeling sorry for yourself . . . you've got to stop. At this point he must say honestly: this death has saved his health, his ability to work, perhaps his life . . . And for that very reason the death carries in itself an especially fertile germ of repentance. Repentance – remorse† – is not yet a spiritual luxury. Only, one must not make it an excuse for intellectual idleness. But he will come back to the question of repentance.

As for the attractive, warmth-giving images of his past life, they were the very things that could no longer be. Those people eating a snack and chatting in the lamp-light, in the way that he wanted them, could no longer be. Not because there'd be no more lamps, or people, or snacks. But because there could never again be that aunt who was the centre of the whole image – animated, fussing, getting slightly in everyone's way but generally liked by everyone, the successful product of his hands. Now, instead, there would always be the dreadful old woman hobbling around half deaf. It was hard to understand this, but he had to. There was no way now of returning to anything good in his life with his aunt. There was only the burden. But he would bear and bear the burden, he wanted to bear it for an infinitely long time, risking his life and risking all the sufferings. Not from love but from an egoistic fear of remorse.

* *Istoshchenie* – literally "emaciation", often translated as "exhaustion".
† *Raskaianie* may be translated by either of these words; here both are offered; elsewhere one or the other, most often "remorse".

The question of himself had got to be sidelined, removed. It was not important enough. And, after all, it was not possible to distinguish in himself the pain of loss from the gnawing torment of remorse. If that torment were eliminated – it's hard to say what would remain of the loss. And anyway, most of the images that disturbed his memory only *seemed* to be images of desire, the desire to go back; they were largely fictions of desire, born of remorse. Their purpose was to exacerbate and maintain for as long as possible the painful sensation of things done wrong.

The question of himself and what he had lost was obscure, false and definitely secondary. The central question remained that of the other person. Of the person who had been deprived of life. Otter did not think that the orgy of death, the millions of deaths we lived in the midst of at that time, had in principle altered anything in our attitude to the fact. Of course it produced indifference, habit, a dulling of emotion, but these need not in the least affect the importance of the fact. A doctor's sympathy for human suffering and death is professionally dulled, too, but it doesn't follow that he has to see his patient's death as unimportant. Millions of deaths (the quantitative factor) are terrible only if the death of one person is terrible. If that *one* has no special importance then neither have the millions. It just becomes all the more true that millions of deaths cannot alter one's attitude to the fact.

Besides, Otter had a deep inner resistance to the current formula: "Now that so many blossoming young lives are being lost all around us, is it worth . . .?" Or: ". . . so many valuable, needed lives . . ."

Being a born sceptic, Otter did not know exactly what made a life valuable and needed. Or by whom it was *needed*. Only some unshakeable idea of a hierarchy of values, supported by absolutes, could help answer that question. Otter had no such idea. But without that – to be honest – he only knew that every person had a sensation of their own right to existence

147

and that everyone had an intuitively understandable right to that sensation. Otter was still relatively young, his vocation was to write [something significant];* and he had the will to fulfil this vocation, a will that nothing had yet broken. Aunt was an old woman; in all her life she had never done anything at all, had essentially loved very little. Now she was useless, a burden. But Otter, after all, is a sceptic and, in drawing up his difficult inner accounts with the deceased woman, he cannot say, even to console himself: "My life is more needed and therefore your life had to be sacrificed." More needed by whom? To those who will read what he will write? . . . But *why* – for what purpose – is it necessary that they should need it? Because he has a direct, empirically given, feeling that the objective embodiment of his thoughts is valuable. Yet his aunt, in just the same way, had a direct feeling of her right to existence. And he had a direct feeling that he, as a blood relative, was duty-bound to support his aunt's life, unneeded by anyone though it was, even if this damaged his own objectively valuable life. And any divergence from this duty was straight away punished by remorse. With the aid of what criteria can a sceptic establish a hierarchy of all these intuitions and direct moral givens? He can only say that the life of a human being is needed by that human being himself, and that people are equal in having a right to existence. In the last months of her life Aunt came alive again every morning in order to receive a certain number of gustatory sensations in the course of the day. Otter, besides gustatory pleasures, received certain intellectual pleasures which, however, were more like hard work. The question of objective value, and of being needed, remained unanswerable, and to act on it was meaningless.

* The verb "to write" occurs here in its perfective form, suggesting a following predicative noun or phrase. As the author, who left the story unfinished, may have thought of coming back to this, the words in square brackets are a guess at what she might have added at this point.

Moreover, Aunt's right to existence was undoubtedly no less than that of other people. So the question came down to what kind of existence it was. Here, too, opportunities for all kinds of cheating were revealed. Otter always disliked conversations in which it was said that someone had "died at the right time", death had "been a merciful release", and the like. In such conversations, those close to the dead person invariably had a secret desire for their own lives to be made easier by the loss, and for the loss to be made easier by that kind of talk. Otter considered it was the person concerned who generally saw the matter most clearly, and being alive meant that the will to live had not dried up. He already knew that suffering rarely kills the will to live (except in the case of a fleeting emotion and attempted suicide), but that there does exist a gradual fading or evaporating of the will, the tending of life towards a minimal level, then its reduction to almost zero. Dystrophy* has taught us the spectacle of gradual, undiverging, and finally easy, annihilation of a human being, a process in which the final act no longer has any special significance. And the troubling enigma of this process (the slow disintegration of a person) consists in the fact that we don't even know at what moment we should weep over our dear ones. Maybe we should have wept for them on 22 June†. Nor what Aunt's existence was like just before her death, and how much life was still in her then, confirmed by her will for it to continue.

Here again, so as not to get muddled but to be systematic and to overcome this heavy oppression, he had to separate out three elements. Her existence in the former life; her existence

* See the note to *Notes from the Blockade* p. 5. In the translation of "A Story of Pity and Cruelty", *distrofiia* is rendered most often as "dystrophy", but occasionally as "malnutrition", "starvation", "physical weakness", "extreme hunger".
† 22 June, 1941 was the day German forces attacked the Soviet Union and the day Molotov (the People's Commissar of Foreign Affairs) made his famous radio announcement.

as it was shaped in the period of the "breathing space"; and, thirdly, her existence as it began to be defined in the most recent time and how it would be conclusively defined that winter. All these had to be distinguished in the confusion of images (of ideas) floating up and troubling his memory.

The first element was, on the whole, positive. In the case of the old man, a person of little energy, in whose life, ever since it became hampered, it was very hard to recall anything good. But with Aunt it was the opposite: you could recall any number of good, amusing, light-hearted moments. Even though all of it tended to superficiality. Meanwhile, at the other extreme, all those lightweight, frivolous and irrational aspects weighed heavily on Otter's life. In any case, Aunt, with her vigour, her capacity for resistance, her invariable wish to have pleasure and to push aside everything unpleasant, was able to get joy from life, and for this reason her life could be arranged with the limited means at their disposal. And Otter arranged it. That life proceeded with interruptions. There was not enough money, Otter was irritable and gloomy. But on the whole it was what she needed. It was a somewhat bohemian life, with amusements and with a minimum of obligations. Her obligations and her activity were like games, they were fictional. She insisted on them because they kept her occupied, and yet all of it could have been either done or not done. Life was arranged in such a way that she did not need to put effort into it. She put in just the amount of effort that would obtain pleasure for her. She visited people, went to concerts at the Literary Club. This pleased Otter. It pleased him when people told him his aunt was a miracle of vitality and youthfulness. Her frivolous lifestyle was his creation.

And now he had firmly to accept that that lifestyle had come to an irreversible end. Both because restoral of such a lifestyle was a matter for the distant, unearthly future, and – mainly – because the person adapted to that lifestyle had ceased to be. "Dystrophy" annihilated her long before death did so. In this

150

sense Aunt should have been mourned, not when she lay dead on Otter's writing desk, but at some elusive, much earlier, moment. But Otter, like most people of the blockade, did not know how to mourn persons who were alive. Too much time, effort, anger and grief were being swallowed up by keeping them alive.

The second element was the pattern of everyday life which had been formed in the "breathing-space" period. In it there was a lot that was terrible: the ever-worsening breakdown and chaos of things, the grime which clung to her body more and more densely (previously she had been very clean), the days spent in silence and loneliness. But there were "one's little joys", as Aunt straightforwardly called them. Whatever the circumstances, a person preserves certain long-habitual personal qualities, and she went on sieving out joy from things as before. It was understandable that, in the present circumstances, the small joys were reduced to matters of food (to which in the past she had been more or less indifferent). She had to endure a great deal of suffering because of hunger; but there really were some pleasures as well. Otter was good at arranging these. Every day there was something for her to look forward to. And for that kind of person does it matter what their childish expectation consists of – whether it's going on a visit, or having cocoa with sweets in the evening? The food mania which possessed Otter at that time helped her take an interest in life. He busied himself with preparing the food, stayed home for its sake, discussed the menu with her. On this basis they made friends. Apart from that her usual habit was to talk about matters which irritated him. Once she said suddenly: "Food is the only thing I can talk to you about. You are in a good mood then. Otherwise you are always bad-tempered." He didn't argue, feeling ashamed of himself. Everything he cooked she found [tasty].* They had

* The sentence was unfinished by the author. The word "tasty" was supplied by the editors as a guess at the missing word.

food festivals (parcels). And nearly every day he triumphantly brought something back. Then Aunt was delighted and he was good-tempered. For he was softened by her well-being (it was his creation – and he admired it), whereas her sufferings, which he could not stop, sent him into an impotent rage.

But this pattern of life which had somehow become settled (here begins the third element, subject to further dividing up) belonged to the summer "breathing space". By the winter, everything was to be changed in a terrible way. With her frivolousness, she did not understand all that awaited her. She relied on him to arrange something. And he was going cold from fear. Yet already, well in advance, she herself began to change in a terrible way, growing less and less fit for any way of life at all. She was losing her memory, going deaf, gradually losing the use of her legs. There could be no going back now, not only to the person she had been in her past life, but even to the person of the summer "breathing space". Some third thing was starting; which still might possibly come about. To pull her through all the hardships to a new summer; to accept her as something new – a person in whom everything was slowly fading away, while resistance and the will to live were fading away in parallel. No longer would it be possible to bring her back to anything at all. All he could do would be to wash her, put clean clothes on her, save her from everything difficult, put her to bed, feed her with tasty food. He would have wanted to do all that; he really would have wanted to; it was one of the few things he would want. And it could not be. But he did set about putting the material in order – material which had heaped up in his memory. He had got to put it in order and not keep on repeating "My poor dear, oh my poor, poor dear . . ."

Wash, reassure, feed with tasty foods – this would be a victory, one of the million human victories over the world's evil which are still to be won by the millions of people who

152

manage to preserve those who have become their responsibility. But when would that happen, and how much of her would it be possible to preserve up to that time?

Even now, nothing will make Otter say the words he was being consoled with: "Death has been a merciful release for her," and so on. Life is life, with all its rights. But the life she had lost was undoubtedly a life of extremely limited possibilities, already tending towards zero. And this made death simpler and easier.

Otter was proud of the fact that his aunt had survived the winter. That too was his work. He liked it when people mentioned it to him, expressing surprise that he had managed to preserve her. And now that the misfortune had happened he felt humiliated, and was ashamed of it. And remarkably, Aunt, who loved feeling superior to others, had herself been proud of being alive and had felt that feeling of superiority over others when she heard accounts of their deaths – especially over elderly people with whom she could compare herself .

There was so much vitality in her that Otter had been sure she would live for a long time yet. But "eternal youth" could not actually continue for ever. Otter was painfully afraid of two things for her – he feared she would be conscious of dying – and it would have to be an experience of sheer horror and of clinging to life as it disappeared; and he feared the crucial moment – which of course would have to come – the moment of becoming senile, of entering into the condition in which no frivolousness can help you not notice what is happening. Up to now, however, she held her position. At 75 she was surprised and hurt when she was called a grandmother (although she was already a great-grandmother). A woman had offered her a seat in the tram (she loved narrating such things) and had said: "Sit down, Granny." With embarrassment she explained that it was "Well, a simple woman, you know . . ." At 75 she complained that she was beginning

to go completely grey. Otter imagined with fear how she would face the approach of senility. He made a mistake, usual in such cases, miscalculating about the fact that the mental dying away proceeds in parallel with the physical. That the first grey hairs and wrinkles may be a tragedy for a woman, while the onset of senility can scarcely be a tragedy. But in Aunt the will to live was so exceptionally strong that in her case the process could be very painful.

In fact everything happened quite differently from how it should have done. Indeed it is probable that death always, or nearly always, comes differently.

The will to live was dying away gradually, in accordance with the developing dystrophic process. When complaining, particularly about Otter's rudeness, she would say: "How afraid I used to be of everything, even of these bombings. And now I'm not. I don't value such a life in any case." She really was not afraid. But her explanation was untrue. It was fatigue, not suffering, that took away the reflexes of self-preservation. The exhausted body's need, by now unconquerable, for peace and immobility.

The body was degenerating, and from habit she was ashamed of this. She avoided looking in the mirror, but sometimes she did look and would say: "How terrible I've become, even my ears have grown long and transparent like a dog's." Or: "For some reason my hair has all fallen out. There's very little left." She felt ashamed, from habit. When alone, she was miserable, yet she was ashamed when with other people. For her it would have been horrible to meet her friends. To some extent it consoled her to think that all those friends were having a bad time too, and that they looked awful. This feeling of shame was largely the reason for her stubbornly refusing to be evacuated to her family. There was a sister there who was almost deaf, and to whom she had always felt immensely superior. And now she herself would

arrive there half deaf, helpless. This whole set of feelings she expressed only in passing, with the phrase: "If they saw me now they wouldn't recognize me." She was far less shy about the fact that she could scarcely control her legs any more, but was ashamed of deafness as a social degradation, as a loss of the possibility of equal rights in communication with others. And now the memory of the lifelong despised inferior sister (they had not even managed to marry her off) was a deciding factor. By habit she was shy and she repressed this fact, and she still did not agree to being deaf. She would say to Otter: "The way you speak, you can't be understood. You keep mumbling." And when Otter rudely and irritably raised his voice, for her to hear it, she found this more insulting than any other rudeness of his. "Why are you shouting? I can't hear anything then . . ." (a pretence, as that was just when she did hear) . . . "Speak normally, but clearly."

Their neighbour would drop in. In other circumstances this would have been a big diversion. But now conversation on equal terms was impossible for her. When the neighbour left she would ask Otter what Anna Mikhailovna had been saying. "When she talks to you, she talks so quietly that one can't understand a thing."

The truth is, she could talk only with Otter, who spoke in a special way. And he thought: "This is how our life has turned out now, but what will happen if she has to go back to conversing with other people?"

She was shy from habit, yet it was no longer a tragedy. The main thing was that she was helped by a substitution of motives: she let herself be aware of what was happening, not as the natural approach of senility, which she did not accept, but as a "dystrophic" illness, something that from her point of view was temporary and transient. After all, what was happening to her was happening (even more) to young, healthy people all around them. So it was not a matter of

her being old. This made her feel better. And she felt better because it was a universal phenomenon. Thus at the time of the revolution, for example, people calmly accepted the loss of their property; the very same people for whom in ordinary conditions it would have been a terrible catastrophe.

So she entered into senility supported by a set of substitute motivations which helped her avoid understanding that the process taking place in her was irremediable and final. She entered into senility prematurely and in a way that was objectively catastrophic and terrible, while inwardly it was subjectively alleviated. She approached death in the same way, with her will to existence being gradually effaced. And this death was unconscious. There were, though, certain symptoms, certain moments that caused Otter a painful doubt. Suppose, after all, she understood, at a time when she could no longer speak . . . Tensely he went through the symptoms, thought up proofs for and against, and could not decide . . .

In any case, it was what is usually called an unconscious death, an easy death. In any case, there was no crying out before dying, no clinging to life. It was a dystrophic death, without excessive noise. There were plenty of gloomy details connected with it – lice, rags, a grave in exchange for vodka, a cart. (Incidentally, Otter considered that, compared with the main thing – the ending of a human life – the posthumous details had no significance.) But the death itself was not dreadful. In itself it was less dreadful than many other things. Less so than what he had done and not done, less so than everything he was guilty of.

And again, going round the circle of ideas accumulated in his memory, Otter gets stuck at the same point, the eternal limit for all egoists who have lost someone close to them – the question of his own guilt and remorse.

Again it was a knot from which strands led in different directions. Tracking and following them, unpicking this knot, one could, again, go far and deep. Once again one could

156

arrive at radical contradictions in life and death, at concepts of time, social bonds, pleasure and suffering . . . But there was no sense in describing this circle for a second time.*

Some things were now clear, in advance. Thus he now knew that it is unjust to accuse people of mourning their dead while failing to value the living. It was not a matter of unintelligible thoughtlessness, it was a radical alteration of impulses. In most cases people do not have really bad feelings towards their near and dear. The bad feeling that possesses them is a transient irritation, continually reborn on the same basis. In the absence of the dear person the irritation is inactive, so then the kind feelings felt towards them become active without any hindrance – including remorse, and regret for one's rudeness – since at that moment there are no impulses towards rudeness and it is inwardly incomprehensible. And now the absence has become permanent. Irritation has ceased for ever, regret and remorse have become irreparable. The entire complex spreads out to infinity.

Something else, too, was clear in advance: the question of the end, the final impression. Otter already knew that what chiefly torments someone who is close to the dying person and burdened with guilt is the thought of a sad ending, of a last impression that cannot be removed or erased by subsequent impressions. In Aunt's life there had been difficult periods (though of course not as difficult as this one) and to them Otter felt fairly indifferent, both then and now; they were cancelled by what came later. But this one would never be cancelled by anything. Yet Otter now knew that, for a consciousness deprived of any clear principle of social connection, this torment was an aberration. For a deceased person, especially if the death was an unconscious one (a person dying while conscious somehow watches himself from

* The author treats these topics in her 1930s narratives "The Thought that Drew a Circle" and "Delusion of the Will".

the side), the sequence of life's experiences is of no importance. One experience in the sequence had simply turned out to be the last. But someone standing nearby, bearing guilt and responsibility, constantly constructs that other's life. And for him the last, irretrievable moment (the completion, the denouement) is filled with awful significance.

These are now the preconditions, given in advance. The rest has yet to be made sense of.

Aunt died from exhaustion. She was done for by the coming of the cold weather, by work that had become too much for her, by a multitude of separate cruel facts of existence. He was answerable for her life, had been arranging it and had failed to preserve it. Consequently it was his fault, his weakness, his humiliation. To have preserved her in the given circumstances would have been difficult, but probably not impossible. With his profound belief in the unlimited possibilities of human wanting, Otter could never have answered such a question in the negative. He ought to have really wanted, ought to have thought hard, worked hard at preserving that life. Then it would not have been impossible. But everything that happened – happened in a world of hyperbolic literalities. To preserve someone else's life meant sharing; sharing a piece of bread; *literally* sharing a piece of bread. One gram more to the other, one gram less to oneself. Every calorie added to the other's share was one less for his own life. The calculation was precise.

Materially, physically, he had done a lot. He had given up the most at the very hardest time – the time of the 125 and 200 grams.* In those days he used to divide the single meal they had, often giving himself only the soup. He was not yet pierced by greed, so it was easier for him. Then came the time of wider possibilities, when human wanting no longer

* 125 grams of bread per day was the allowance for a dependant from 20 November to 25 December 1941; 200 grams from 25 December 1941 to 11 February 1942; even according to these norms the issue of bread was irregular in the first half of January.

needed to sacrifice itself blindly, but could achieve a great deal. And he achieved a great deal. He stood in queues and he cooked, he carried dishes and tins, he managed to get extra items through privilege (this was something else Aunt could be proud of as showing their superiority over other people). At all periods of that year, he was head of the family, the organizer of life. The one who transferred the sole serving of porridge from his plate into a plastic box; the one who later dragged a heavy Moscow parcel in a pillow case – not given to all, only to those who performed some official function – containing chocolate, rusks, butter and preserves. As he dragged it he was choking with impatience to reveal it and surprise her as quickly as possible; at the same time thinking: How stupid it will be if I get killed by a shell now. He was the one who triumphantly unwrapped a salmon issued on meat coupons in the canteen. – "And they say people in Leningrad are starving . . ."

All of this was a kind of "self-realization"* and it interested him. Also, it was something taken for granted. At first he was

* The Russian noun *realizàtsiia*, which transliterates English or French "realization", occurs sixteen times in the story with the meaning of "self-realization", "self-actualization", perhaps also "self-presentation", "performance of self" or "achievement of personality". It seemed appropriate to keep, where possible, the author's own word, thus it has mainly been rendered as "self-realization" or "self-realizing".

In her notebooks, however, Lydia Ginzburg often uses related concepts, mostly with a prefix meaning "self-", "oneself", such as *samo-utverzhdenie* (self-affirmation, self-assertion) and *samo-opredelenie* (self-definition), as well as *avtokontseptsiia* (auto-conception, self-conception), and in the story she mentions the sense of *samo-tsennost* (self-value, value as a person). Accordingly, on a few occasions in the translation, *self-affirmation* and "self-assertion" have been used to translate *realizatsiia*.

As a psychological writer and a reader of contemporary psychological theory, Ginzburg was especially interested in studying how people worked at, and asserted, their personality (realizing that which they experienced as a value) in the conditions of a given society, and

not even aware that he was giving up what was his *own*; he simply distributed whatever – all of it taken together – was allotted to the family unit. Much later he had a chance conversation with P.F., a woman gifted with splendid abilities for self-preservation. He told her of his household arrangements and she said abruptly: "I don't understand these enormous efforts to save the life of a seventy-five-year-old person." "What do you mean? What should one do with that person, then?" "Well, I don't know. But it's always at your expense . . ."

They parted and Otter felt with displeasure that the conversation had got into him and was leading him to new ways of thinking. He suddenly realized, for the first time, that he was not so much distributing as re-distributing. That the family unit contained two unequal magnitudes: a worker's ration book and a dependant's one; and the coupons in the worker's book stood for *his* flour, *his* fat, which he could have consumed but instead was re-distributing. That stupid conversation was thus the beginning of an inner protest, and afterwards Otter always disliked coming across P.F. It was especially unpleasant now. Part of his guilt belonged to her. To that self-satisfied female who did not even lose weight during the blockade.

He still continued doing what in general had to be done, remaining, as he had to, on the level of head of the family.

particularly how some learnt to do so even in the terrible conditions of the blockade.

To give two examples of the word *realizatsiia* in the story: (i) At the point to which this note is appended, Otter recognizes that his enthusiasm for obtaining the daily food for himself and his aunt and for keeping domestic tasks under control is actually the process of his own "self-realization" as "head of the family"; (ii) throughout the second half of the story, his verbal violence against his aunt is an attempt to impede and to crush her own attempts at establishing her value as a person – her *realizatsiia*.

This was the current norm of behaviour and he did not drop below it. He shared – though not completely. He left more bread for himself (according to the norm), although Aunt always longed for bread so much. But he too suffered from the bread psychosis. It seemed to him he would not be able to live and work without it. On the whole he was eating more. Aunt enjoyed repeating: "You need it more." It was true: he did intellectual work, he ran around in circles, he dragged buckets and chopped wood. That was all so, and yet it was obvious that she had needed more as, after all, she had died. Besides this, he did some things that were crafty and unconscientious, he allowed himself to cheat in small ways. In that epoch of wider possibilities, when he was doing the dividing up at home, he would often conceal the fact that he had already had an extra porridge at the canteen, and still took more for himself. He shared the sweet foods he had been given at lunch-time. But sometimes, unable to resist, he would eat them all, then lie that he had not been given any that day. Sometimes he lied again the next day, saying that to make up for it they had handed out a double portion, and he gave her all of it, but sometimes he cheated. Yet she had such a childish desire for the sweets, which she used to cut into tiny pieces with a knife. To cheat on sweets was a cruelty. He would shout at Aunt, saying she drank too much and it was bad for her, ruinous. But other times he gave in and brought a whole lot of the soup or coffee she wanted, secretly thinking, with a bad conscience, that if she ate plenty of soup (which she liked) he could more easily give himself extra porridge or bread.

More could have been done. Perhaps she could have been saved. But in the world of terrible literalities, in which all this was taking place, that would have meant putting his own life at stake. The passing of coupons from one member of the family to another was a dangerous and visible process, like a blood transfusion. Somewhere there was a limit – fatal or irreparably destructive for the one giving blood.

161

It was the same with work – with the question of taking on an extra part of the domestic work. Factually and physically, he doesn't have the time to do so, as he is tired out by those same domestic tasks; if he is to spend still more time on them, he won't be able to work and earn money – and the two of them will perish. This argument was not false, but it lay on the surface. In the depths there was, once again – blood-transfusion. To take more upon himself – after which he would inevitably have to take on yet more, and yet more – meant going right up to the limit beyond which began the direct sacrifice of his life. This Otter did not want. Not because he wanted to assert that his own life was more valuable, and so on. But direct sacrifice of his life he did not want; he didn't feel it to be obligatory. He was inconsistent, because towards the moment of Aunt's death he himself was physically very unwell. And everything that was happening was essentially a process of gradual self-destruction – which, by chance, her death interrupted. But it was precisely a gradual, not especially noticeable, process, composed of many small habitual actions which one by one took their place in the circular daily rush, so that by now it was impossible to remove them or to replace them with something else. It was all being composed of trifles which were inalienable and were taken for granted, and in the end it turned out to be just that: self-destruction. Everything was accomplished without any sort of heroics. On the contrary – with a continual feeling of shame for one's rudeness and cruel violence; with the sense that all of it was "sharing though not completely" and that he was nonetheless cheating for his own benefit. But direct sacrifice of his life, intentional and planned in advance, was not something he was going to do, nor did he feel that he ought to.

This is why the main weight of guilt lay not on what he did or did not do that year, but on the way in which everything was happening.

162

In the world of literalities, the world where plain meanings took the place of all the metaphorical meanings, her life's dependence upon him had also become absolutely literal. She was helpless: if for two days he failed to bring her a meal she would die. Never had responsibility for another's life been so great. It was the responsibility of a mother for a nursing baby. Otter knew he had saved that life – partly at cost to himself – and yet he himself had poisoned and perhaps destroyed it. Everything was dreadfully material: grams, calories, drops of blood. Everything was decided by very concrete and very individual matters. Like in a desert, where you can save someone's life by giving him a gulp of water and can kill him by withholding it.

And he had poisoned it not by any psychological subtleties but simply by horrible rudeness and bad temper.

How could all this have happened?

It was like a continuation of the old quarrel between them. Aunt possessed all the characteristics that irritated Otter, plus an astonishing lack of ability to relate to him. It was actually very easy to mollify him by giving in, but she never gave in. In short, it was an old quarrel in which he was always rude and uncontrolled. But then helplessness and dependence did not yet have their literal meaning at that time. In blockade existence this quarrel was to become something quite formidable, and indeed it did; like everything else around them, it was in essence already a quarrel about life and death.

Otter was unhappy, ill, embittered. Above all, he was worn out, running in a circle. People were all in the same situation, all were monstrously unrestrained and out of control. On the street you couldn't ask someone the time or how to get somewhere. In answer you would receive only abuse. Especially terrible were women in queues. As they waited, they were impatiently, voluptuously, looking forward to being asked a question by someone, so that they could shout and swear at

that person as he deserved. Everyone had a reason for their indecent behaviour, just as drunks used to. In all sorts of ways they exploited the excuse of extreme hunger, for the removal of social constraints lightened the load that pressed upon them.

Otter was doing as everyone did. He was in any case generally inclined to a lack of discipline. All his will power, all abilities for self-control, went into one thing only: his work. In everything else he was lazy and unconcerned, and, as he preferred to spend the least possible mental energy on everything else, he just left it to go on as it had to.

Otter was embittered because he was unhappy in general, and because, in particular, he was unhappy about his aunt. He was unhappy because of her very existence, which had created the conditions for that trap of everyday life into which he had fallen. And he was unhappy because she was unhappy and he could do nothing to help.

Her life – which was his successful achievement – had been spoilt for him, and from this he impotently suffered. He could not bear anything which reminded him of it. And when she complained (she had begun to complain, which was a sign of degradation, quite new and therefore especially noticeable) he would fly into a rage and shout that she was ungrateful, spoiled, that she had things which few others had, things she did not even deserve. To him her complaints were an insult, a denial of his endeavours and achievements. The shout was meant to muffle his feeling of desperate helplessnesss. He got angry because it was easier to live with anger than with pity. He could get on well with her when she was cheerful and playing at being a young person who did nothing – the finished product of his hands. But it was hard to behave well towards what was happening now. To do so, he would need either love, which had gradually disappeared in his indifference, or adherence to a principle, a firm sense of duty, such as he had never had in his life. Instead of all that, he had an empirical sympathy and a

sense of their being blood relations, as well as the unclarified inertia of a certain average level of behaviour. Love or conscious duty – these were a matter of self-realization, and sacrifices made sense in relation to them. But in relation to the "inertia" level of behaviour, sacrifices only made you feel oppressed and angry.

A definitive expression of this anger in words might have been subject to the customary prohibitions of courtesy. But courtesy, already largely ruined by everything that was happening, was dealt a final blow by the extraordinarily stubborn – and for her, fateful – resistance which Aunt put up to all Otter's wishes. This old opposition*[16] turned tragic in the given circumstances.

With his utmost strength Otter began his battle with chaos, the battle for rationally aware existence and creative work. The more successful the forms taken by this battle and the more opportunities it had, the more he was enraged by all that hindered it. In the worst time of all, the "125 grams" period, Otter was relatively gentle and patient. All that mattered then were instinctive attempts to save his own life and, at the same time, the life close to his. And although these were in fact mutually contradictory tasks, in practice they merged into a single effort. But when it was a matter of creative work and of getting free time, all the contradictions became prominent. Domestic life was tearing his time out of him by the roots and he was furious. He was battling with chaos purposefully now. He was busy solving problems of rationalization and of routine. And all his efforts were obstructed by his aunt, the incarnation of chaos, personification of the irrational, the muddled and the absurd. Every unnecessary movement cost him terrible mental and physical

* Here the author adds the parenthetical phrase "(reference to earlier composition)", which probably refers to her sketches and character analyses for the unfinished work *Home and the World* from the 1930s (located in her archive), in which Aunt was a central figure.

efforts and he fell into indescribable despair by her causing him to make these efforts for nothing. The basic absurdity was that she did it from a desire to be kind; there was no ill will at all. It was absurdity, fundamental irrationality, and it led to a maximum of fury. He was beside himself when she broke crockery, spilt or dropped valuable bits and pieces of food, straight after he had insistently asked her not to pour either liquids or grains from one container to another, and so on and so on. He flew into a rage not only because of the dystrophic greed, but also because what was being destroyed was his whole cherished and careful construction of the most rational use of time and resources. Time was being torn out of him by the roots. Aunt would complain and say: "In the winter, when life was so hard, you weren't so angry. When I said it was hard for you to lug those tins around, you used to say: 'If only there were something that needed lugging.' And now you're angry all the time . . ."

It was true. But then, in the winter, he had not been trying to work and think and to free up his time. Then, all he was doing was instinctively trying to save two lives, and he was glad of anything that might serve that one purpose. Whereas now he was fighting against chaos, and Aunt was the avant-garde of chaos. She was a living, animated particle of chaos, which was why he could vent upon her all his hostility and anger. He had entered open battle with the avant-garde of chaos and of a world of enmity. He encountered his aunt's boundless and insuperable obstinacy. Complete inflexibility towards his requests, persuasions, explanations, oaths, threats. He knew that nothing would help, even if he were to smash himself to pieces against this wall. And the great obstinacy of chaos, deadly for them both in the circumstances, drove him to an extreme degree of now almost permanent embitterment, releasing him from the social prohibitions, from all the delays of pity, courtesy, decency, or simply civilized habits

166

(in any case the customs of civilization were cracking apart all around them).

He struggled. And here again he made a mistake. There was in fact nothing to struggle against. It was impossible to overpower with one's own stubbornness, impossible to alter or rectify anything. Impossible to go away or to give up, because of the responsibility and the blood relationship. There was no one to take revenge on, because you can only take revenge on hostility, on ill will which can humiliate you. But there was no ill will, and he could not be humiliated by anything coming from a creature absolutely dependent on him. In a word, there was nothing to struggle for, and *no one to struggle with*. It was like the meaningless way we punish inanimate objects which cause us harm yet have no evil intention, like kicking a chair across the room when we've bruised ourself on it, or violently slamming down the telephone receiver when it takes a long time to answer. These actions are senseless, but it is hard not to do them, as they provide a discharge of emotion. The same thing was happening here. Expressing anger in words gave relief. Removal of constraints was an enormous relief. For prohibitions weighed especially heavily on the moral habits of dystrophic everyday life. And, in such a destabilized situation, absolving yourself from prohibitions was enough for you to set out immediately on a path of unlimited, utterly dissipated unrestraint.

Once the prohibitions were removed in principle, they could be removed further and further. The more they fell away, the greater the discharge and the relief. Everything which people of a certain level of civilization have to keep to themselves, repress and work through – the irritation, the reproaches – all of it could now be discharged. A particular, exceptional relief is gained from making reproaches, as it is particularly hard to keep quiet about sacrifices one has made. Thus it came about that little by little (it had already become customary)

the most terrible words were spoken. Terrible words of all kinds – oaths, reproaches, threats, demands, curses. In his speech two abusive terms now became regular; they seemed to apply to everything and he used them constantly. They had become the standard form in which he automatically reacted to anything absurd that came from her, anything chaotic, contrary to common sense or to accepted behavioural norms. From abuse to reproaches there was a natural transition. "So I've wasted my health and my life for the sake of such a cheap thing as you." Incidentally, whenever he spoke of his health and life he felt he was using mere clichés of reproach and anger, but in fact they were quite close to the reality. As he said these things he felt a blind animal relief from the prohibitions that oppressed him, and he kept count of all the sacrifices he had made, all the deprivations he had suffered because of her: the chance of going away, a hospital, better food (for he couldn't leave her on her own, nor could he leave her with her dependant's ration book). There was a time when he had renounced these advantages more or less indifferently, but now he avidly tracked them all down, seeking what else he could discharge his resentment upon. He looked in all directions for the most crude and dreadful things to say, the worst things possible, as though only the utmost grossness could calm him and be equal to the burden that oppressed him. He called her a parasite ("You squander everything that I've bought with my own blood. You've been pouring tea into the slop-pail, thinking it was some kind of slops. Because you just can't stop poking your nose in where you're not invited. I forbid myself to eat the last piece of fat – I bring it home – and I find it lying on the floor, all trodden on. Just when I'd begged you not to touch it or move it. And the main thing is, you're not the least upset about it. That's the attitude of a parasite accustomed all her life to having everything served up nicely cooked.") He did not conceal how irritated he was by her deafness and by the way she couldn't control her legs.

("Stop that! It's easier for me to serve you than to watch you hobbling about. You can't take two steps without grabbing hold of things and poking your nose in. The result is everything's on the floor.") He would threaten her unbelievably rudely: "Okay, so I shan't bring you dinner for two days, *then* you'll have to reckon with me. I'll teach you to reckon with me. Oh yes, I shall. What you need is a punch in the belly. Since you don't understand any human speech."

In this way, removing one prohibition after another, he talked himself to the point he was bound to reach – the most terrible point, that of talking about her death. When she brought out the usual cliché – "I won't be a burden to you for much longer" – he would reply: "Hm, we don't know yet about that. More likely you'll drive me into my grave first. Judging by how I feel, living the life you've set up for me. And when I kick the bucket you'll really be in a tight spot. *Then* you'll know what it's like with your dependant's ration book." Or he would say: "I'm not the least bit worried about you" (which was untrue, he *was* worried about her) – "people like you don't give up the ghost. It's the good people who die" (incredible, incomprehensible, how he could say this). And finally he reached the limit. It seems he said – this is so unbelievable that there is even some hope he may not have said it after all – "If only you *would* die at last . . . Going on living like this is impossible." And that was a few days before her death. Apparently he did say it. Shouting it so loudly she seems not to have heard it. Which means *no one* heard it. In which case it is the same as if it had not been said, but had remained merely a bad thought. But that's a trick. The truth is, he did say the most terrible things. He, a person who had experienced reality through words, and feared words; he, a custodian of verbal chastity.

How, indeed, could all this have happened? He was indifferent, irritable, uncontrolled. But, after all, he was not

bestially cruel. He had always found it hard to cause pain. His will power instantly weakened if it met with someone else's suffering. Aunt used to say to him: "You're nice to everyone, only not to me." It is a common characteristic of weak, undisciplined persons who cast off social prohibitions when they are at home. But it was not only that. He would reply to her (and it was true): "From everyone else I can get free, and I do so the moment they become repulsive to me. But from you I cannot." From everyone else he was in fact fully protected by his indifference. But here indifference could not be complete because of responsibility. In his search for other means of self-protection, he found the most ugly ones.

He was not a cruel beast, and the things enumerated here would not have been enough to make all this happen. Two further factors were involved, two unfortunate aberrations.

The first was that, through inertia, he had kept his long-held conviction that Aunt's power of resistance, her vital force, her "realizing" of her personality, were indestructible. This had nothing in common with, say, the old man's frail affirmation of himself, which could be damaged by the slightest incautious movement. It had long been Otter's habit to oppose (to impede) Aunt's "realization". Firstly, because this habit was an outlet for the irritation her stubbornness and self-satisfaction caused him; secondly, because he saw in this a means of self-defence against the imperialistic tendencies of her "realization", which threatened to overwhelm everything around her. Always, therefore (not only when in a rage), he said things to her which were wholly forbidden by the laws of courtesy. He regarded this as proper educational method and as a means of self-defence against this life force that had overwhelmed him. He had gladly tried, for example, to impress upon her that, while being on the best possible terms with her, he did not in the least need her. That in his household there was actually nothing for her to do, that he did not need to be looked after, and that she should live for her own pleasure as far as

possible, with which he would assist in every possible way. – Meanwhile, one of her favourite playful notions was that she lived not for herself but for them, her nephews. This was part of her "self-realizing" and he tried to destroy it without the least pang of conscience, since he considered that in any case nothing could destroy those playful notions which – for her own pleasure – she might want to keep as her right.

In the new conditions he continued struggling against her attempts at self-realization. And in the world of terrible literalities this struggle acquired a monstrous character, as did all struggles. As before, it seemed to him necessary to go on with the cruel struggle, it was even *especially* necessary because now her stubbornness and self-satisfaction, her reluctance to take account of, and obey, reasonable advice (now crockery was broken, food knocked onto the floor, paraffin spilt) meant the final breakdown of their wretched way of life. If she were distressed, if she felt repentance, then of course he would be sorry for her and perhaps would himself try to console her. But it was remarkable how little she cared about the losses from which she was the one who physically suffered. It really was the psychology of a person who is not trying to obtain anything, who has never in her life sought to obtain anything, certain that she'll receive her due (little though it may be) in all circumstances. The sole thing that concerned her was that she should not be in the wrong, as if nothing mattered except the question of her guilt or innocence. Against all appearances, she maintained that she never broke any crockery. Or – that it used to happen when her hands had grown very weak, but now they were somewhat stronger. "And anyway, a certain amount of crockery always gets broken, for every housewife – you should see how much crockery M.L. broke when I lived with them. Something broke every time. And how calmly she took it." And if the subject of spilled grains came up, Aunt would provide a precise and detailed set of reasons as to why it had happened. It would

appear that essentially it couldn't have *not* happened. Otter was especially enraged by the way she argued about the piece of fat (brought back by him from the canteen), which he had looked for and then found trampled on the floor. He had asked Aunt not to take it out of the tin box he had carried it home in. But she for some reason decided it was necessary to take it out, which of course she did the moment he went away. Didn't notice she had dropped it, looked around for it, then forgot it. About this there was a terrible shouting scene ("bought with my blood . . poured down the drain by you . . . !"). But Aunt explained it had all happened because she had wanted to keep that piece for him – for Otter. It was incomprehensible why that meant she had to take it out of the tin. "All this cursed motherliness," she said.

No, she did not wish to give up her self-assertion. And he considered that their wretched way of life, hanging by a thread as it was, required protection, although of course there was more involuntary irritation in his reactions than calculation.

And he dealt with her self-assertion in a terrible way: on all sides he searched for whatever could possibly undermine her sense of her own value. He had found the word *parasite*. He was not afraid of the words "invalid", "cripple" ("You've crippled yourself at my cost so as to send me to my grave, once and for all"). He picked out two coarse, disparaging expressions which, in his opinion, best expressed what was happening – "squandering" and "filth". He used them all the time, in all contexts. He called it "filth" when she soiled the bucket which stood in the room because she could not wait till she got to the lavatory; again it was "filth" when the food was prepared badly, when she licked her plate, when she added water to the porridge he brought from the canteen so as to make more of it, like a soup ("Go on, do what filth you like. It's actually disgusting to bring you things, as you make everything filthy"), and when she didn't dry the bread

172

properly and said "I'm only warming it." Otter was incensed by this stupidity. He sought out her sore spots, and when he was especially angry he would tell her that her favourite, V, couldn't care less about her, had loaded everything onto him, was a swine who didn't think it necessary to send money but just flung it at her when he had any left over. ("He's a marvellous character, though. And I, too, would be a marvellous character, if I were hundreds of miles away from you.") The V theme was a cleverly discovered sore spot; she scarcely uttered any objections. With malice he ripped and trampled her self-affirmation, and he told obvious untruths, exaggerating all the bad and hiding all the good that he felt. He said he didn't care a rap, only everything that happened to her was at his cost, and if he went to any trouble for her it was to save his own life. He concealed the fact that he nonetheless needed her, that she was his last protection against nocturnal loneliness, that she was the home and living soul without which life was hard. Carried away by the battle with her "realization", he kept silent about that. And this keeping silent was the cruellest of all the things he did. Even crueller, perhaps, than the shouting and the scenes of rage.

But in all this there was a mistake. An irremediable miscalculation. It was the aberration by force of which we don't want to notice, and we *don't* notice, the fatal alterations in our near and dear ones as they approach death. Through inertia and old memories Otter thought he was dealing with that same indestructible self-realization which ought not to be spared. Whereas in reality she was already undermined by degradation, by those ears as transparent as a dog's. She was already close to confessing herself an old woman and to having doubts. Stubbornness, opposition, assertion of her own righteousness – all this still remained. But it was all, perhaps, only a surface now, something she persuaded herself of. Beneath that surface other tragic processes were already taking place, and something of them came through to

173

the outside and could be glimpsed. He was stamping on the already fragile constructions she might have been using her last bit of strength to maintain while desperately putting off the moment when it must all crash down into degradation, the final loss of all her value as a person.

This (the indestructibility of her self-realization) was one of the aberrations which soothed his conscience and allowed him to remove the prohibitions.

The other was related to it. This consisted in his certainty that Aunt was not a real person and all her life's reactions were mere games, fictions. The only exceptions were the simplest physical reactions, which Otter considered it his duty to satisfy. In all else, in everything involving words, he could allow himself unrestraint, because words and ideas did not provoke real human reactions. That meant he could allow himself the pleasure of removing the prohibitions without fear of seriously harming a human being. Otter had had a similar relationship with Lialia.* He had convinced himself, once and for all, that her reactions were playful fictions and in consequence he had been strangely cruel to her.

As for Aunt, there were grounds for such a conception. She was so asocial, so ingrained with moral parasitism, that even very personal impulses failed to function in her if they demanded some sort of social expression. One such personal–social complex was interest in one's family, which was surprisingly reduced in her case. It meant nothing to her that she was a grandmother and great-grandmother (except in that she was ashamed of it), nor had it even begun to enter her consciousness that her granddaughter's husband had apparently perished and that the situation there was terribly difficult. She went on talking about his bad manners and his way of pickling mushrooms, as if everything were continuing

* Ginzburg refers to earlier works of her own: Lialia is the name of Otter's romantic partner in several of her narratives from the 1930s.

just as before. When there were no letters from V for a long time she said she was dreadfully worried, but it was clear to Otter that people (when they love someone) don't express their anxiety like that. She could not worry in a real way, focusing on the object of the worry, because she could not go beyond the limits of each given moment, which of course kept being filled with its own, *other*, content. When Otter came home and told her a shell had just exploded two paces away from him, she gave a ready-made reply: "Just imagine, I felt somehow uneasy all day today." But he saw that it had not got through to her at all because the moment when the shell exploded near him and the moment when he told her about it were two different moments, which for her could not be connected. The present moment had its own content – anticipation of the meal Otter had brought. Yet once, just before May 1st,* he had joined a queue for beer and had stood there nearly the entire night. He supposed that, as usual, she would not be worried, but when he got back she was trembling all over. She said straight out that she thought something had happened to him and she was thinking of what would become of her now. For in this case a section of time, a moment lasting all night, was filled with the immediate and tangible content of his absence, absence of the person who, in the most literal sense of the word, fed her from his own hands (a dog's longing for its master) – quite a different matter from the abstract lack of letters from a distant town. Generally, if something did happen to him, or he felt less well than usual, Otter did not in the least need to conceal or soften the fact. She remained cool and composed. Indeed, he not only didn't conceal it, he emphasized it, thus extolling his own sacrifices.

This absence of natural human reactions served as justification for the total removal of prohibitions. He was vaguely

* May 1st marked an important national holiday in the Soviet Union: International Workers' Day.

aware that in relation to her he should avoid only such cruel actions as would materially deprive her of something. And he did avoid those actions. Despite his threats he continued going out for things and lugging them home and enthusiastically thinking up various additional items of food for her. She knew she needn't worry about what he did, and she made use of this. Words, though, belonged to a special category, on the other side of reality. In this way a certain ludic fiction came into being on his side, too, a kind of terrible word game with nothing barred. This was aggravated by his constant feeling that he could not say seriously words which for him had always been the words of the most savage people, those on the lowest level of civilization. He had seen those people from a distance – in the street, in the pub, in shops – and he had read about them. Their shameless vocabulary was a psychological fact which he found it interesting to try to understand theoretically, but which could have nothing in common with his own psychological possibilities. This feeling of, as it were, theatrical alienation from his own speech, a kind of stylized imitation of something, was strengthened by the fact that he was using not his own words but ready-made standard formulas known to be steeped in all the vileness of philistine cynicism. Such were those set phrases: "you're driving me to an early grave, you've made yourself an invalid at my expense, you look after number one all right, don't you?" These phrases had gained a settled form because they perfectly expressed a nasty perception of life which was not, however, his. So a two-sided game was bound to develop: words that were not of one's own making, and reactions that were not real. This playing is surely a transient thing, the product of a dark area of life, something which will later have to be either driven beneath, or forced out of, one's consciousness. Aided by the absence of witnesses.

But in fact it all turned out quite differently. The game of terrible words proved to be the final impression, and therefore

176

of an indestructible [. . .]* game, with use of symbols from another category.

A deed meant something which deprived her of certain material benefits, and this deed he did not do; he did just the opposite. What he did was not an immediate continuation of the terrible words cut off from reality. But it was in fact a deed, and probably a crime. For he failed to consider – in his deranged state he forgot – the medical side of the question. After all, peace and quiet had been prescribed for her in their former life.†

Perhaps all this was one of those family crimes which are hidden deeply and for ever. And he must have not fully understood this as yet, for if he had he would obviously have had to react in some other way.

All the significance, all the horror, all the depth and weight, of what has happened has not got through to him. He doesn't feel himself branded a scoundrel and a murderer. He forgets about that. He now allows himself moral judgments, normal responses to reality, kind feelings, human relations with people. Sometimes he remembers – "The truth is, I'm a criminal and I have lost for ever the right to all that." But this awareness skims over the surface and slides away. The will cannot pin it down, has not the power to do so. By making use of the fact that there are no witnesses to the crime, no moral censure or judgment from outside, such as would have objectivized the guilt, the mind's mechanism has not made that awareness its own. Were it to do so, it would be impossible to live as though nothing had happened.

Yet terrible scenes arise in his memory at odd moments, as if shoved there by some kind of elusive mental jolts. In a rage he throws her down onto the sofa, and even though he is no longer touching her she shrieks and flounders, waves her

* There is a break in the original text at this point.
† i.e. before the blockade.

arms and jerks her poor rag-covered feet about. On top of all the rags, fur slippers have been dragged, patchy and bristly with what has remained of their fur, and tied underneath with ribbons (once they were his own good house-slippers, brought to him from Murmansk). And he shouts in disgust: "Stop squealing like a pig. Shut up, or I won't be answerable for what I do. I can't bear the sound of your loathsome voice." There were many scenes of this sort.

To some extent he was right in his loutish calculation that she had no genuine human reactions. In each separate incident her reaction turned out to be non-genuine. Nonetheless, in the last analysis he was mistaken. By his behaviour he had created a certain general, average tone – the tone of their unhappy shared life. And its main quality got across to her. For him this tone was created above all as the precipitate of a multitude of shredded, vanishing moments. The things he irresponsibly shouted at any given moment, himself not believing what he was saying, disappeared along with that particular fit, but between the fits of irritation there remained a continuing link, for he kept himself constantly in the atmosphere of screams and rudeness, with an alert readiness to break out into rage at the least movement or word.

Only occasionally, in the evening (for in the morning he was always bad-tempered now, as that was when he had a clear head and he wanted to work and think, and couldn't because of their way of life), when he had eaten, and knew that Aunt had eaten, he would sit there tired and softened and discuss the menu with her or the likely prospects of the next distribution of food. He would say: "You're eating quite well now, you really are. It's time for you to put on some weight. You are still so very thin." And Aunt would sigh over her thinness and agree that she was eating fairly well. This pleased Otter and immediately tamed his temper. But those were just moments of respite. Shouting relieved him psychologically, as a discharge of tension, though at

178

the same time it was bad for his weakening body. When he shouted, his temples swelled and throbbed and his heart hurt. He felt it was harmful, and felt he was losing the last of his valuable strength – a foolish loss because what lay ahead for him was the task of making rational sense of his life. This made him still angrier and, because she was to blame for his having to shout, he shouted all the more violently. In the past his custom had been to flare up and then quickly calm down. As soon as he became calm he felt ashamed, sorry, and so on, because, as with all hot-tempered people who don't bear grudges, the impulses that move them once they have flared up cease to be *understandable* immediately afterwards, and are therefore straight away replaced by other, even opposite, impulses. For they are purely affective impulses, real only while the feeling lasts. Outside it, one ceases to *understand* the reasons and objects of one's irritation, just as one ceases to *understand* toothache when the tooth stops aching. One is then ashamed of one's bad temper and coarseness and promises oneself it will not happen again, for it now seems easy to hold it in check. It's only a matter of not uttering that first sharp word which set it all going. But now something new had begun to happen to him, something which had never happened before in his life. The intervals between outbursts were becoming so short that, in those intervals, he no longer lost his understanding of the bad-temper impulses.

He hadn't time to lose the understanding. The anger passed, but the understanding of the impulses remained. This led to a kind of middling state of embitterment, completely new to him. For a while he even liked it. It gave him a sort of satisfaction which he explained to himself in this way: to do something vile, repent every time, then do the vile thing again, is a most unworthy occupation; whereas to preserve an embitterment while feeling calm is proof of his innocence and of Aunt's guilt. To his surprise he found that now, after a domestic row, he could go nearly the whole way to his place

of work still angrily remembering that the food jars had once again not been prepared and that once again he had wasted time, strength and nerves on this. In actuality the embitterment had become stable just because he was always unhappy and oppressed by the mundane side of life. But when he searched for self-justification it seemed to him that his cruel behaviour proved his rightness – he was deranged enough to regard his own cruelty as proof that he was in the right, for (as he said to himself) he could not be as cruel as he was (in relatively calm moments) for no reason at all. Sometimes he maintained his anger and indifference when Aunt was complaining and crying, even though he was one of those people who can't endure someone else's tears. At those times he deliberately said to himself, in so many words: "She does it on purpose, to make me pity her. It's a pretence. And if I'm able to take this view of the matter it must mean that she really did drive me to . . ." With indifference he listened when [. . .]*

In his settled embitterment he reached the point at which he did what he himself considered "deeds". Once, when the jars had not been prepared, he returned home leaving something behind – not actually on purpose but because there had really been nothing that could be taken without a jar. But he told her this with malicious joy. Once, when they had had a big quarrel, he told her that he was going off to work even though there was really nothing for him to do there, and that he would try to return as late as possible – "Just so as not to hear your loathsome howling". (The phrase "stop howling!" and altogether the word "howl," were now used by him as frequently as "squandering" and "filth".) She did not want to be left alone in the dark and began piteously begging him to stay and make it up, despite the fact that she tended to bear grudges and he had just been outrageously rude to her. All the same he went off triumphant and spiteful, slamming the

* Another break in the text.

door behind him. He did not turn back when he reached the staircase. Yet the truth is that he did not return very late. In his understanding, this was already a "deed". And the fact that he had become capable of cruel deeds in relation to his aunt was for him unexpected and surprising, a confirmation of her guilt.

But there were times when something unforeseen would suddenly touch his heart with pity, pain, shame. He would sometimes sit on a small bench beside the stove, listening absentmindedly to what Aunt was saying from her sofa. She would be saying that there were no letters from V, that she wanted to go into hospital, or else that he, Otter, had become such a bad-tempered person.

"You hate me, and it's understandable, since you make enormous sacrifices because of me . . . I never hear a kind word."

And suddenly what she was saying would somehow tear through the heavy fog of their everyday life, reaching him not with its particular content but as a general sensation of life as one long misery (previously she had been so good at getting joy from life). In short: that sensation had been created by him. Aunt even spoke of it directly. "It's still summer. And the food is good. We could live. But you are so irritable, so irritable."

Other individual things came across to him, too. Once he was sitting by the stove, tired and wanting to stay silent. And Aunt started talking about something unnecessary. And he, with his usual readiness for irritation, had already asked, sharply: "What do you mean by that, then? Why do you say that?" when she suddenly replied: "I mean just that. After all, I've spent the whole day in silence, like in prison. I simply want to talk a bit." Among her usual false and long-winded explanations this was such an unexpectedly clear truth that Otter's heart missed a beat from sadness. However, he no longer had any kind words for her. He said nothing.

Another time, after a big row, he returned in the evening in a gentle mood. They had tea together and chatted pleasantly. And Aunt suddenly said: "When you went away I had a good long cry." He had been telling her, more fully than usual, that she was a parasite and had spoilt his life, and so on. Usually, when she replied with "What you're saying just finishes me off, it makes me not want to live any more," etc. he remained indifferent. But, this time, the words "I had a good long cry" turned his heart over. It was not said in order to make him pity her – he was already in a gentle mood. It was the truth. It turned his heart over that she could cry after he had gone out. Not for show. This straight away changed the meaning of her tears. It meant she did have real human reactions. It meant that, in his negating those reactions in order to calm himself he had gone too far, perhaps gone the wrong way altogether. Thus doubts and sorrows arose, to be rapidly washed away by the next bout of irritation.

So he was sometimes ashamed. He was ashamed when she thanked him for doing something for her, or called him by affectionate names, and said "darling". It seemed to him that sort of thing was impossible after his savage, ugly rudeness. And that she was creeping up to him, knowing well her total dependence upon him. This thought made him ashamed and gloomy and he could not look at her.

And again it is painfully necessary for him to remember what it was, after all, that led him to those horrid states of rage. What they started from every time, in exact detail. In search of self-justification, striving to lighten his guilt if only by loading part of it onto the dead woman, he again analyses her character. This character, in various contexts, has already been subject to more than one analysis. It is such a consistent, complete character, so fully expressive of certain psychological tendencies, that there is a kind of monumentality in it. In any case, it was deserving of study.

What can Otter say to justify himself (but is it really a justification)? That she was a bad person. Undoubtedly she

was a bad person. An absolutely finished product of a parasitic way of being (a lady) – an asocial and amoral person (for all morality is social) in whom even the basic human feelings had atrophied. She was a bad person, unkind and harsh wherever she felt she could be harsh in relation to what was weaker than herself. This cruelty [sic!*]was due not to any desire to cause evil but to the fact that, in her mental machinery, momentary egoistic impulses encountered no obstacles whatsoever. She did not do any (great) real evil, only because she was ill-adapted to doing anything at all; ill-adapted to performing any objective acts which would change reality. But in a passive way she was cold-bloodedly able to cause a lot of evil. Otter himself knew the whole gamut of bad and petty motives. But he, with his intuition of goodness and of values, was horrified by frankness, epic straightforwardness, in the expression of them. As if it were a terrible immorality, he was horrified by the way everything which ought to be hidden, ousted, prohibited, everything that lived within himself as a shameful secret – all of it, in her case, came to the surface with extraordinary ease, passing naturally and imperceptibly from thought to word and from word to actions. Whereas, for him, between those stages in the transfer of evil there lay gulfs. All those manifestations of egoism, vanity, cupidity, envy, all the ingratiating of oneself with the powerful and oppressing of the weak – which for him were difficult and secret – flowed along in her mind with extraordinary ease and directness, being no more than the function of a desire to receive as much pleasure from life as possible at every given moment. And Otter felt this easiness and directness to be deeply immoral.

* In Russian, the words for "harshness" (*zhestkost'*) and "cruelty" (*zhestokost'*) are just one letter apart, and thus Ginzburg's use of the latter is an apparent slip of the pen.

Yes, she was a bad person, and at the same time a very charming one, much liked by all who knew her slightly without having to share their existence with her.

She was magnificent in her gaiety, in her unfading and indestructible affirmation of life, in the likeable absurdities and naïvetés which she had carried through a hard life and which were dreadfully oppressive for everyday existence, although to outsiders they were amusing – something she knew and played on. He remembered, now, that he had undervalued that charm, of which there was a lot, including the physical attractiveness that had lasted for so long (not for nothing did she enjoy great success despite having never been pretty). And it was not boring to be with her, even for him. What irritated him so much, what he called by the horrid word "fool" – was actually not stupidity, it was absurdity due to a social impotence, an astonishing lack of practical and correct ideas. In general, though, her mind was quick, capable of games and of certain entertaining constructions. Thus she was able to tell interesting stories from her past (always the same ones, it's true). These long-past stories did not require checking against practice and common sense and were therefore successful. He never once told her this, however, although it would have pleased her. The truth was that, with half-conscious cruelty, he avoided everything that might have strengthened her sense of personal value.

Along with the easy, direct way evil was manifested, there was the sphere of hypocrisy (for this, too, Otter had found a lasting name: "sanctimoniousness"). This was her system of attributing good, noble qualities and motives to herself. Really, it was not even hypocrisy. For one thing, it was too regularly combined with the system of unconcealed evil – that is, of unconcealed immorality. Two assertions could thus co-exist, and did in fact splendidly co-habit: on the one hand the assertion (her life-wisdom) that one must derive profit from people. I can profit from everyone: this is good. On the

184

other hand the assertion of her own goodness and disinterested benevolence: this is good, too.

One or other of these assertions was selected according to which one of them, at any given moment, was better suited to having the pleasant experience of asserting her personal value. (It is good to be clever and it is good to be kind.)

Secondly, this hypocrisy system did not in the least aspire to deception (especially deception with practical significance), or to the disorientation of people around her. One could speak of a disorientation of outsiders, yet it was precisely in relation to outsiders that it was used more carefully. And it crashed down upon Otter, who got irritated and continually unmasked it, and in whose case there could be no question of his being deceived. For this reason it was not hypocrisy (with its practical tendency) but was merely the playing of a game that provided a specific pleasure.

Not a good character, indeed. Like most characters in that period, it preserved and exaggerated its basic qualities when it was applied to new material. If Aunt had always sought to feel superior to others wherever possible – to feel, for example, better catered for than solitary old women, etc. – she had the same feeling now in a form corresponding to the present circumstances: she was proud of not being an outcast with her dependant's ration card, she was proud of Otter's privileged purchases or the financial help from V. Whereas the son of one friend of hers didn't care a fig for his mother and, what's more, that son later died of starvation. Another lost her husband before the war and now she was left with a dependant's ration card. True, she had a lot of good things to sell, while Aunt was left with nothing but rags. But even selling very good things gave far fewer grounds for praise and for feeling superior than did the privileged dinner Otter received. For in the privileged dinner there was an element of recognition and special favour. She was proud of that, and was even proud of the fact that she had not died.

Aunt had preserved her basic qualities, and had preserved her attitude to Otter, which he considered a bad one and which was the basic point in his self-justification. Painfully he continued drawing up his accounts with the dead woman. Of course she was attached to him, but only within the limits of her egoism and her need for activities and amusements. She had always made use of him for her fictive games, or else simply for practical purposes when she had to give reasons to her relatives for leaving or staying, and so on. If she wanted to stay in Moscow it turned out that she was sacrificing herself because he liked living alone and she didn't want to disturb his peace. If she wanted the opposite it turned out that Otter could not do without her help in his household, so once again she was sacrificing herself. No amount of protesting made any difference. Never did she consider *him*, his tastes, habits, desires, his work or his leisure. She did not consider him because he never impressed her and because, despite all his shouting, she was not afraid of him – not afraid, that is, that he would do any *deed* which would be to her detriment. Nor did she need to try to win him over, since she knew that he himself would do everything necessary for her welfare. And all this applied fully to the present situation, only in monstrously magnified and accentuated form. Despite the fact that her dependence on Otter had become absolute and literal, she still failed, as before, to take him into consideration; despite his violent behaviour, she was not afraid of him. He relied on that, and what for him was particularly unaccustomed and repulsive was the suspicion that if she spoke affectionately to him she did it on purpose, to ingratiate herself. However, his suspicion was probably mistaken. For she said to him, once, in the same direct way in which she sometimes suddenly said certain awkward things amid her usual falsity – "I'm not in the least afraid of you. You shout and swear and attack me. But I'm not afraid of you, and I'm not angry with you. I can't be angry with you. I'm soft-hearted." And from there the playful

186

fictions continued. This no longer mattered. Otter mumbled: "It's a pity you're not afraid: it would be better for us both if you were." All the same, it made him calm down.

The principle of her attitude to Otter and all her lifelong characteristics were carried over by her into the world of terrible literalities in which they now lived. And in this world those characteristics became terrible. Particular characteristics gave rise to particular collisions, invariably self-renewing, dully repeatable. In their clenched and cramped way of life a precise norm was worked out for quarrels and clashes: they had several types of row. At their base lay the several complexes of her characteristics. The complex of stubbornness (interwoven, incidentally, with all the others), the complex of frivolity, the complex of inattention, the complex of muddle-headedness, the complex of hypocrisy. These, and the brawls related to them, even became tied to particular functions of daily life, and thus to particular hours of the day. Behind all these complexes stood one fundamental one – a consciousness that was torn up into self-sufficient moments, each one of which was seen by that consciousness as the source of possible pleasure, received instantly. This frivolity, this non-attention, this mental muddle (all of them shaped by social parasitism). And it is the maximum of stubbornness, for every action is taken according to a momentary hedonistic impulse, with no regard for that connection and interrelation of things which rational conviction requires. Therefore no rational conviction can reach that divided-up consciousness.

In the world of terrible literalities each one of these complexes seemed to Otter catastrophic, threatening him with ruin. And he waged a cruel, crude and desperate battle against them which over-taxed his strength and was utterly unavailing. For against him stood a monumental, irrational, elemental *obstinacy*, which was moved by a dark intuition of immediate satisfaction of desires and against which all conviction, entreaty and anger were powerless.

For instance, every time he had to get ready to go to work and at the same time take with him the jars for their dinner – the complex of inattention came into force. It would turn out that the lids were not ready and the string bag had to be looked for. This was repeated day after day, despite requests and promises. It drove him to despair.* The person who was supposed to help was instead being a hindrance. Rationalization was destroyed. It began with the lid being in the wrong place, then it became shouting on the theme of inattention – "And I've spent my life and health on such ungrateful trash! . . . I can't get you to do even the slightest thing! . . . All your life you've thought only of yourself, and it's what you're doing now." The complex of hypocrisy came into force at meal times, when Aunt invariably denied herself food for Otter's sake, but in an extremely uncertain and unconvincing way; or else she did eat but made excuses for doing so. And he was angry because it pleased him when she ate what he brought. He considered that all this ought to happen somehow differently. And he would shout the standard formula he had worked out: "Stop these sanctimonious charades!" The same complex made its appearance in the mornings, when Aunt wanted to stay in bed but pretended she was about to get up . . . With the falsehood complex Otter mostly clashed in the evenings when he came home to find that various things had gone wrong during

* Ginzburg preserved the following variant of the beginning of this paragraph:
"Every day when they washed the dishes he begged her to collect and set aside the jars and lids needed for [fetching] their dinner. And every day he again had to extricate it from chaos. This sent him into a frenzy. It began as a practical fight against stubborn, torpid chaos. The difficulties of daily living had now become so acute that sometimes immediate measures had to be taken against torpor, for a torpor which will not submit to verbal persuasion meant that the stove had gone out, the food was spoilt, and altogether there were irremediable disasters."

188

the day and had to be concealed from him. Then he would shout: "Don't lie about it, just don't tell lies!" She would say: "Why don't you believe me?' – and he would shout: "Believe you! Your whole life long you have never spoken a word of truth!" Stubbornness was always there in everything: it could not be picked out. Muddle-headedness was that entire wrong conception of things, so typical of an asocial, parasitic consciousness, and the tearing apart of moments from each other so that they could not be connected. Whereas sound thinking consists in the right inter-connecting of moments. But now this had become a catastrophe – it meant that she put the tinned meats in a frying pan on the hot stove to heat up for him on his return but had also got the thermos on, so they burnt to a cinder. He would shout about her squandering crumbs (crumbs he had paid for with his own blood), and about how he had allowed himself to eat only a tiny piece of tinned meat and it had been so tasty, so nice, and now . . .

One aspect of the complex of frivolity stood out for Otter as the most catastrophic: her carelessness, which in the case of even a really slight illness was replaced by the cruellest hypochondria. This came from the fact that at every moment she lived the content of that moment only. In one, the content was health (therefore illness was unimaginable); in another, it was illness (so recovery was unimaginable). The possibility of Aunt's falling ill hung over Otter like a dreadful threat. But he knew that if she wanted to wash in cold water she would still wash herself, or mop the floor, next to the buckets, then walk about with wet feet. He'd shout: "Aunt! Haven't you caused me enough worry! Now you want to fall ill as well, just to destroy me and finally send me to an early grave! . . ." More than anything else, their rows were about unboiled water. From somewhere Aunt had got the idea stuck in her head that you should not heat water to boiling point but only up to sixty degrees, at which point all bacteria were supposed to die (she liked the scientific sound of that). And however

much Otter raged she still drank, and gave him to drink, that unboiled "sixty degrees" water, assuring him that today the kettle had boiled like mad. He could have turned white and fainted, he could have been smashed to smithereens – nothing would change her. In reply to all his shouts Aunt would say: "So far I have not fallen ill. M.L., when I lived with them, was quite insane about boiling the water. And she got one stomach trouble after another. So that has nothing to do with it." Nothing was more calculated to drive Otter mad. He shouted: "Will you understand! You'll be the death of us! It may be all right once, all right a hundred times, but at the hundred and first you'll fall ill. And this is a time when we must not, *not*, be ill . . ." But he knew shouting was useless, he could shout himself blue in the face and the water would still be heated to sixty degrees because that killed the bacteria. And beneath his cracked, almost extinguished, shout he would repeat: "How I hate you . . ."

He had got used to the way all the troubles of their domestic life were Aunt's fault, caused by her stubbornness. In particular, the destruction of her health. If she caught a cold, she was to blame for not taking his advice and for wiping the floor instead of waiting for him to come home and wipe it himself. But of course she needed to play the victim and the self-denying mother, so as to torment him even more later on. In the summer he said to her: "You must go out every day, or you will lose the use of your legs." She did not obey him but waited for weather in which it was practically impossible for her to go out, and her legs did not work, so then everything was altogether his fault. From morning to evening he repeated: "Don't drink, don't drink more than you need." But it was like throwing a pea against a wall, and now she would swell up, and so on.

It was a great relief to him to be able to shout and accuse her of her own sufferings, rather than be tormented by pity. These accusations were, above all, a splendid justification and

190

pretext for not being bound by any requirements of courtesy and for keeping his freedom to reproach her as before. She was to blame, and so he could reproach her for swelling up, for going deaf, for losing the use of her legs, for turning herself into a wreck – all because she had not listened to him, and all of it a misfortune for him. From inertia and habit, and in order to justify himself, he still went on and on accusing her, and now he was accusing her of having died.

Yet nothing helped. She was his sole blood relation. Love had evaporated along with much else that was human. But the link remained, the responsibility remained, and so, therefore, did the pain of pity. He pitied neither kind people nor powerful ones. Nobody. He pitied only a terrible tormented old woman who had poisoned his life and nearly destroyed him. Whose life he had saved and then, probably, ruined. He did not pity anyone else.

Connected with this death there was another aberration, the most important one. We are always in the power of aberrations when it is a matter of our near and dear ones, towards whom we are guilty. Because through various mental tricks we try to get rid of the guilt or to justify it.

The aberration (a protective one, adduced against his own conscience) consisted in the way Otter continued to regard his aunt's behaviour as a regular – only magnified – development of her lifelong characteristics, whereas in actual fact it was all moving on into new, pre-death, symptoms.

She broke crockery, she dropped and spilt things. Without any need she would pick up the large saucepan full of coffee. And Otter would not have time to say "don't touch it" – the coffee was already pouring onto the floor. He would be angry and would think it a continuation of her usual muddle-headedness and lack of coordination in her movements – but already this was a stiffening of her hands and feet. She forgot everything, mixed things up, and he thought it her usual

absurdity, whereas it was loss of memory and the sign of approaching dystrophic and senile dementia.

He had understood nothing. Yet now new symptoms were appearing, quite unlike any previous ones, symptoms which would certainly have revealed the truth to him if he had at all wished to see it. She began complaining and talking about her unhappy life: this was the loss of her power of resistance and of the protective optimism which had hitherto never failed her. Suddenly she began using Jewish intonations of lament. In general there was nothing especially Jewish about her character and Otter liked to repeat a sentence he'd thought up: that her psychology was not that of a Jewish lady but that of a lady landowner undergoing ruin. He called her plaintive intonations "wailing"; they offended and irritated him, as evidence that he could not organize her life.

Once he was heating soya milk for her on the stove – something she liked very much. And Aunt suddenly said, in the mourning intonation – "Oy, if only they would give us this milk . . ." "Oy!" he teased her. "Anyone would think you never saw any. Thank goodness, they give it to us every day. Why wail?" And she replied, with the suddenly lucid understanding that always disarmed him: "I know. It's just that I've got this way of talking now."

But the newest symptom of all, which overturned everything, was that she stopped fussing about, and kept needing to lie down. This was such a contradiction of her essential psychology that it would undoubtedly have led Otter to the awful truth if it hadn't, instead, led to his being absorbed in egoistic thoughts about the breakdown of their way of life.

The death process was gradual and it was hard to mark where it began. At the start of the famine Aunt had still possessed her frivolity and her indestructible optimism. She endured well because she had reserves of her own fat and because she always ate little and did not understand much about food. She had always liked foods that were sweet and

liquid (and cheap, besides). Now she enjoyed standing in queues at some sort of "cafeterias" to get sweetened coffee and syrup, which at home she would convert to a jelly. Otter calmly left her to obtain food for herself in the cafeterias. In that period he did not grasp the awfulness of her position, just as he did not grasp that of his own.

Then Aunt fell ill, with flu or angina. Otter was cross because it was owing to her own carelessness and meant trouble for him. He then started sharing his dinner with her. This was the beginning of suffering and the beginning of understanding. Aunt's illness was a crisis moment, for afterwards it was impossible to resume the naïve idyll of the cafeterias. The terrible way of life began. And came to a head with enormous rapidity. Each day everything got worse – hunger, cold, darkness, descent into wildness, mad hurry. Otter was absorbed in the struggle for himself and for Aunt. Every minute was directly defined by the preceding one, by the demands and sufferings stored up in the preceding moment. Nothing could be linked together or summed up. Because of this, Otter did not notice the changes taking place in his aunt. The culmination of the terrible way of life was approaching. When there was no more firewood, and Otter left home, and Aunt found shelter with a starving neighbour who treated her badly. And after a few days, to Otter's surprise, she was found lying in the neighbour's freezing room, under blankets and a coat, too weak to get up. He pulled her out (quick! quick!) and with effort dragged her to some friends, where she stayed. This was a kind of respite and things became clearer. It seemed Aunt was scarcely able to go down the stairs and could not go to get bread by herself. This was astonishing to Otter. He said: "Just think! Aunt! In such a condition! Her!" He thought it a psychological trauma, a temporary phenomenon.

Once M.L., at whose place she was staying, said to Otter in the course of a conversation, that his aunt was a very old and very hungry person. For him this was an unpleasant surprise.

He wasn't ready to hear that Aunt was very hungry (nor even that she was very old). Until now she had been satisfied with very little. She had been content when he brought her half his dinner, and now that he was getting a complete dinner for her he thought everything would be all right. He wasn't yet used to tracking changes. But now it seemed that was not enough, and she was going to need more and more.

Towards spring, they returned home. It was the period of the "breathing space". The problem of food had become much easier and Otter was excited by what he could obtain. Aunt shared his enthusiasm. At home she was very active, spending hours working away at the greens from which she cooked a most nourishing porridge. For hours she washed, chopped and boiled the leaves. It could all have been done more simply but, as ever, she would not listen to any argument. The work exhausted her. Otter comforted himself with the thought that without it she would have been miserable. She did not want to go outside. She was no longer used to that. Outside, her own degradation was revealed in ways that displeased her. She felt herself to be a decrepit, hunched old woman who dragged her legs. And her eyes became wet and, in the unaccustomed bright light, soot appeared on them that could not be wiped off. Otter saw all this with sudden clarity on the rare occasions when they went out. And she felt it when they were outside, even if she could not see it. For her the outside was frightening, uncomfortable, embarrassing. Moreover, it was boring. She had always enjoyed going out but only with a purpose, on an errand. It was wrong just to go to a shop for nothing, there were not even any cafeterias any longer, and Otter rudely refused to trust her with the ration cards.

People told Otter she should definitely go out while the weather was warm, otherwise she would lose the use of her legs. He shouted, but didn't really do anything about it. He was afraid she would go off somewhere on her own and

he didn't want the worry of fearing that something would happen without his having had time to make amends and to put things right. And going out together meant dragging oneself along painfully slowly, step by step, pottering along. It was too tedious. And in fact he did not have the time. And Aunt was looking for reasons for not going out. First it was a lost key, and she kept dreaming of the key. Then the key was found, but she did not go out. She thought up a way of putting it: "You don't give me the ration card. Am I to go out like a fool?!" "Yes, you must go out like a fool, otherwise you'll become a complete cripple at my cost . . ." But she went on, ignoring his shout: "I'd be a fool to go, with so much work to do at home. Once I had a sit down in the garden and something happened in the house. And you came rushing . . ." This argument sent Otter into a real frenzy of rage, because it was justification by sacrifice and laid the guilt on him.

It was nearly autumn. Both Aunt and Otter, equally naïvely, thought the food had got better, so the general situation must be getting better. They thought this was happening. But at the same time, certain bad symptoms suddenly appeared, unexpectedly and of a completely new sort. Sores appeared, which were not there before, just as there had never before been the intonations of Jewish grief. Other phenomena began, such as, for example, haemorrhoids. Defecation was extremely painful for her. Sometimes she would tell him she had been screaming when he wasn't there, sometimes he himself heard her groaning as she sat on the bucket. He listened without kindness because he was too tormented to take on this additional pain.

He had always panicked about Aunt's illnesses, treating them as something very serious. Now this could not be done, his running in circles could not be interrupted for the sake of actions not known about in advance. On every occasion he would spend a long time getting ready for such an action (call a doctor, go to the pharmacist) and while he was getting

195

ready the sore place somehow went away by itself. So he got into the habit of thinking, "It will go away!" Thus the sense of catastrophe was numbed.

Another torment she had was an itchy rash. He knew the cause and in bad-tempered moments told her it. But she would not agree with his reason. So measures had to be taken, but to take them was physically too difficult for her (in her time she had always been very clean and tidy). So she said it was not that at all and that she had nettle-rash. And nothing could make her give up this conviction.

But most serious of all was the swelling, the legs. Both he and she should have been alarmed by this, but they were not because they were busy with other things. Otter was busy proving that Aunt herself was to blame as she had not listened to him and had drunk too much. He himself had connived at that and brought her cabbage soup without giving up coupons,* and coffee, because these solved the problem of her nourishment. And Aunt was busy proving that she was not to blame. "Drinking a lot has nothing to do with it. Anna Mikhailovna drinks eight glasses at a time, with no consequences. I've always had this, it's a sign of gout. Now probably of sciatica too." As with the nettle-rash: it was more comforting to have something old and well-known. It was not lice, not dystrophy – results of the terrible new way of life with its threat of uncertainty and death. "Nettle-rash", "sciatica" – that's all it was. So they quarrelled and for both of them the catastrophic truth of what was happening remained hidden. Once Otter came home before nightfall. Aunt was lying on the sofa, all hunched up. She raised her head and he froze with horror when he saw her face, bitten all over and at the same time puffy and squashed from lying

* Employees attached to government-department canteens could receive certain products without giving up coupons from their ration cards. See also p. 19 in *Notes from the Blockade*.

down. "No more liquids!" He felt certain that drastic remedies had to be applied to her. The shouting began. "You've no self-control. You're not a human being. There's nothing human left in you. All you do is pour more and more and more water into your belly. Stuffing yourself with liquid. Look at you. Look at your dreadful swollen face. If you want to know, people with faces like that die within two days." She took fright. After that she drank less for two days, then she considered the swelling had gone and she could gradually start drinking more again.

As winter approached there arose the question of placing Aunt in a hospital. They had influential connections and Aunt was especially pleased by this as an aspect of their privileged position (not on the same level as everyone else). With her lack of social sense she stubbornly went on imagining a hospital to be as it was in the past – something like a private clinic with doctors you knew – just as she still mostly imagined a shop as in the past, remaining convinced that at Yeliseyev's* the goods were superior. For her a hospital was a naïve dream of comfort and rest. She wanted that and was therefore completely indifferent when she was told that people were badly fed there, that there was less food than at home, and that someone would have to bring food in. Otter had himself raised the question, but now he opposed it. Later, to calm his conscience, he found out that it really was very bad there, though at that time he could only presume it was so. He opposed the idea for a number of reasons. He was horrified by the thought of the extra, unaccustomed actions – not belonging, in short, to his routine – which he would have to undertake to get Aunt placed in a hospital. He was against

* A luxury food and wine shop on Nevsky Prospekt (in the centre of Leningrad/Petersburg), founded by millionaire Grigory Yeliseyev in 1910; nationalized by the Soviet government as "Gastronom no. 1", it has always been popularly known as "Yeliseyev's".

solitude (this, out of pedagogic considerations, he would not for anything have mentioned to Aunt), and against the disruption of an established style of living. And above all (the maddest reason!) he was held back by a reluctance to interrupt their shared life at a time of bad, unrectified impressions. Thus he always disliked it when she went away, even though their shared life oppressed him.

It was impossible to confess all this. And he concealed it all with the worst egoistic arguments (which had nothing to do with it). The main thing was that he would have to drag himself the devil knew where to get food to her. Aunt answered with the most altruistic arguments: her chief purpose was to save him from herself. He wouldn't need to drag himself anywhere. Or maybe just once a week. He was enraged by the altruistic tone. The ineradicable frivolousness. Because she wanted to take a bath (actually in those hospitals there were no baths for dystrophic patients) she did not think of the fact that she would be hungry, hungrier than she was now. But it was he who would have to think about it and bear the whole burden of it himself. And he shouted: "Relief? While you exist, there is no relief for me. Ruin me completely – that's more like it! When I'll have to drag myself over to the Petrograd Side every day and bring you everything I've got. Fool that I am, to have given you this idea. Now you've got hold of it and you won't let go."

The question of hospital and of the absolute necessity of somehow looking after Aunt's health got postponed along with many other things that were being postponed from one day to the next. Otter grew used to thinking the sores would somehow resolve themselves. The itch, too, seemed to have gone away (occasionally Aunt said: "Why doesn't it itch while I'm eating?"). Probably the legs would find their solution as well. At that time Otter was particularly irritable, as it was precisely the time when he was carried away by the problems of rationalising their way of life. In the system he

was constructing, Aunt could reasonably be used for work within her powers. Without any parasitism. The time and the strength he spent, the pleasures he forfeited, would then be justified by the benefits to their domestic food and the reduction in domestic hassle. Aunt's illness upset everything. The annoying disruption of his calculations made him furious. His attitude to her lying down (she spent more and more time lying down, saying that then she was warm and free from pain) was not a benevolent one. He began to suspect that lying down was just one more of her *ideas*, like the greasing of her hair with butter to stop it going grey. Deranged by anger and egoism, he (a psychologist!) refused to understand that these were two different things: greasing her hair with butter did not contradict her essential self, whereas lying down did and could only be something she was compelled to do.

The sense of catastrophe was so numbed that he was demanding work from her (even to him it seemed crazy) although any work was too much for her now. "After all, you're not so very ill any more," he'd say, "Get up and help me today." The same scene was enacted every morning. He would take out the buckets, run to get water and bread, prepare breakfast; during this time Aunt was lying in bed. He knew she did not want to get up, and also knew that she certainly would not get up. Yet every morning she found it necessary to start a conversation about whether she should get up, whether there was any sense in getting up, and so on. These were her regular sanctimonious charades. And recently Otter had begun answering quickly and rudely. "Get up. If you please! And fast!" She did not get up.

About the new habit of lying down, which was so strange to him, he got lost in contradictions, since different impulses moved him simultaneously. On the one hand there was pity for her and, especially, fear of a *deed*, for the demand that she do some work was already turning into a deed which could

199

cause her bodily harm. On the other hand there was pity not exactly for himself but for his time, which – by means of all kinds of rationalizing contrivances – he had been saving up for his creative work and which was being ripped out of him as if from his very flesh. He would first shout: "Get up!" then: "Go to bed!" And Aunt, not without some sarcasm, accused him of hypocrisy: "You call me a hypocrite, but you yourself are one when you make me go to bed and then start shouting." He did not reply. Strictly speaking, it was not hypocrisy, it was a clash of heterogeneous impulses.

The same clash of impulses took place in relation to her food. On the one hand, remnants of humane feeling were still active, along with his self-realization as "head of the family" (satisfaction at having organized her life). On the other hand, irritation at the irrational swallowing-up of his strength and resources. Everything proceeded sporadically. Sometimes he would put food on her plate, thoughtfully selecting the nicest pieces for her, at other times he would suddenly burst out with something rude. "Oh, I see you are looking after number one today. You are only supposed to have 300 grams of bread a day. Total lack of discipline. You just want to gollop it all up at once." He was irritated by her system of eating butter in lumps on the pretext that it wouldn't spread. He justified his protests by the fact that the method was not reasonable and he was trying hard to allocate the food rationally; but these explanations were a cover for bad feelings. There were quarrelsome exchanges about the butter which, like all arguments with Aunt, led to nothing. "Why are you watching every move I make? It's quite disgusting." "I'm watching because you are starting to put the butter on in lumps again . . ." Otter considered that butter in lumps or without bread was another of her *ideas* (she had decided it was especially good for her) and that a heightened interest in sweets (she was always calculating how long it would be before the next issue of "confectionery") was a sweet-lover's

old habit. Obtusely he failed to understand the new func-
tion of the phenomenon. By instinct a dying organism avidly
seeks what might save it: fat, sugar.

Sometimes, especially in the evening, in bed, when the
rotation of things had quietened down, Otter had the fleeting
thought: she is dying, she'll die this winter; a new attitude is
needed. But the thought of catastrophe flared up and disap-
peared with elusive speed, engulfed by current self-centred
considerations. It vanished so fast he wasn't able to recall the
contexts in which it arose, to localize it.

Concerning her death the question arises, as it does
concerning her life: what could have been done? Perhaps she
could have been saved, though at an extremely high cost.
But what had to be done now was to comfort, to reassure
and to make arrangements for the process of dying. This too
required enormous exertion, a loss of mental strength. For
this, one had to *understand*. Understand that this was not a
condition that would last for ever. This was the final illness.
One had to tell oneself that this was so and enter into it as
into one's own self-realization. He had understood too late.
Or: he would have had to find love in himself. Perhaps love,
and through love the rescue of this pitiful, closely kindred
life, were worth the price of his cruel creative work. This he
does not know and will never verify. There was no love; there
was nowhere to get it from.

Only now that he can think without haste does he realize
that love was necessary, and that Aunt was not outside
everything genuinely human, in the way it had seemed to
him in his haste. A certain mental life was being lived within
that tormented organism. Perhaps more when she was
asleep, when consciousness was freed from the rushing and
fussing. She dreamt complex, coherent, interesting dreams
which she enjoyed telling to Otter. (She used to say – when
he was going out with the bucket in the morning – "Ah,
there you are, sit down for a minute, I've got a dream for

201

you"); she was proud of them, as one is proud of poems one has written. But Otter listened to them with embarrassment, because in them Aunt's inner mental life became apparent and this demanded attention and sympathy, whereas in his haste he preferred to deny and ignore it. Listening to these dreams was all the more difficult and embarrassing for him because he clearly saw in them the thought of death, which she was afraid of. Once he woke her up because she was groaning; it turned out that she had been having a monstrous tormenting nightmare. She was dying; she lay on the floor, and a broken marble table had fallen onto her chest, and in her hand for some reason she was grasping a bottle. It was a straightforward nightmare, terrible for her but less frightening for Otter than her dreams full of displacements and implications. Thus, not long before the end, she dreamed of her deceased husband and a young man who had shared their communal apartment and was killed at the front. They were arguing about which of them should be first to enter the apartment (this very apartment), and were giving way to each other, and the neighbour's wife, who had died of starvation, was greeting them. And Aunt's husband nonetheless gave way to the young man who, after all, had arrived joyfully to see his family and needed to enter as fast as possible.

For Otter this was a very frightening dream. Aunt now lay for hours on her sofa, saying she was never bored but was thinking. "What are you thinking about?" Otter asked her with the same heavy feeling of embarrassment. "Oh, about you, about myself. But mainly I reminisce. And I'm never bored."

That was a mental life. What he ought to do now was stoop down, pay careful attention, offer consolation. Otter just stayed silent and listened with an uncomfortable feeling. He was tired and found it hard to speak, especially to speak loudly (Aunt by now was hard of hearing); if he was to

converse he preferred it to be about food. That was simple, customary and interesting.

The very last period before the end was a bad time. Not bad as regards food; but very bad as regards Otter's condition and behaviour. His irritation with the chaos that destroys time grew and grew. In the very final days there was an accumulation of certain oppressive and ugly scenes. Aunt had hidden his braces somewhere. He looked for them, thus wasting time, that very same time of which two-thirds were spent on carrying food to *her*. He became frenzied: "Don't poke your nose into things, don't interfere. Leave my things alone. I'll find them, for God's sake. I'll *make* you leave my things alone." She denied her guilt, but she really had hidden the braces, for later he found them lying in a very visible place (obviously put there surreptitiously). For the moment, though, he did what he used to do in such situations. As if he were searching (which was a pretence) he systematically tipped all the contents of the cupboards out onto the floor. Then went off in a rage. She had to pick it all up. He knew that every movement was hard for her now. This was already quite definitely a *deed*.

That scene half-merges into another – concerning trousers that had not been mended. "I've been asking you for a whole month. I've got nothing to go outdoors in. This is impossible. Just get up and do it." She gets up. The room is cold. He goes in and sees her sitting at the table. Shivering in her green cardigan. She's holding the trousers in shaking hands. With horror Otter suddenly notices how terrible all this is. She bends her head down to the table in a kind of oblivion, and her head is trembling, too. Otter's desperate shout: "Go back to bed immediately!" "No, not now you've got me up." He tears the trousers out of her hands. He shouts wildly. How dare she not obey, how dare she prevent him from putting right the wrong he has committed, immediately and as fast as possible.

After that he quietened down. That evening he went to bed early, terribly tired. He asked her if she could put up the blind for the night herself. Aunt went to raise the blind and, coming back, bumped into the bucket. Otter shrieked, hearing the sound of a fall. Embarrassed, Aunt said she was not hurt, but she couldn't stand up on her own. Otter leapt up, lifted her (it was strange to him, to feel how light she was), carried her to the sofa, laid her there, covered her up, conquering his disgust at her sofa and the rags on it, which for some time now he had avoided touching (there were lice). That evening he understood. Accepted the fact: Aunt is seriously ill. And he changed his way of thinking.

They agreed that Aunt would stay in bed. This became law, and immediately things seemed easier to Otter. The following day the food was good. He brought rice pudding. But Aunt had no appetite. That was strange, yet there was something positive in it, a suggestion of peace-time. She had already eaten some soup made from herring heads, rust-coloured. Otter had tried to persuade her not to eat it. – "Look what you've done to yourself!" He said the herring soup had blocked up her stomach. But there were bad signs. She felt sick and longed for something sour. These were signs with bad associations. That day, sugar (a great rarity!) was issued at the canteen. He chopped the sugar into tiny lumps and said to her: "Eat this, eat plenty of it. You need it as a medicine." But Aunt said: "I'm actually glad I have no appetite. There will be more bread left for you." At the shop they announced wine and sprats. She very much wanted some wine. Unexpectedly it turned out that the wine was very expensive (50 roubles) and Otter didn't have enough money on him. He bought sprats and said next day he would receive some money and would get the wine (but next day there was no wine, so she did not have that last drink of the wine she wanted). After a while she suddenly said: "Just think how expensive sprats are – what was it you said? 50 roubles." (Sprats cost 1 rouble

30 kopecks.) Calmly he said that it wasn't the sprats, it was the wine, but he went cold all over. He feared the weak-mindedness which was already approaching and could be lasting. He was frightened and gentle. He said: "In the morning we'll do a clyster" (she liked clysters – this too was one of her *ideas*) "and everything will get better." He kept asking: "Well, how are you feeling? Better?"

In the morning he definitely wanted her to eat the sprats. The last time they were distributed she had liked them very much. One must eat so that the body doesn't get emaciated. And so that Otter's achievements will not be in vain. That morning, occupied with domestic business, Otter paid Aunt little attention. But then he gave her the plate of sliced bread and sprats, and she began fussing at the plate with a trembling hand. A sprat slipped off, he picked it up, again it slipped, and Aunt ate sprat and bread separately, staring meanwhile with a fixed gaze that bore no relation to the food. It was unbearably similar. It was how the old man ate oranges that time.* And in this moment Otter understood everything. He started hurrying. He acted like a fool and a barbarian. He made her eat more than she could, so that the body would not get emaciated. Now he fetched the clyster. She believed in the magic power of clysters. Otter was always unwilling to use it, finding the thing repulsive. He thought she would be pleased this time. But suddenly she said he should not do it, she didn't need it. All of a sudden she became tired, like someone who had just finished some heavy labour and she didn't want to be disturbed. But he

* In "Delusion of the Will," N (in the manuscript he was "Otter") brings oranges to his father when it is already too late. Ginzburg describes painful scenes of the father's eating pieces of orange and later spoonfuls of juice from them after he has already lost full consciousness and the ability to speak. N's belated arrival with oranges haunts him with remorse.

insisted, like a fool and a barbarian. He tried to do it. But now he found he could not turn her over, her body was heavy and cold as stone, with distended abdomen. She was falling asleep. And nothing came of the clyster. He merely got everything wet all around them. She fell asleep, paying no attention. He could not lift her, or put dry things under her. He now knew that all was lost. And everything took its course, more and more quickly. There was a sense of delirium, as with that other death, only in an accelerated, compressed and simplified form. Immediately, their neighbour made her appearance, as if there were a law of nature that she should. Though previously it had been quite impossible to expect or request anything of her. Straight away there began a changing of clothes on the stiffening body, and various operations which were no longer needed by this body and had been so greatly needed by it just a short while ago when it was alive and perceptive. Then, however, it had received no relief, it was left in dirt, rags and lice, and it *itched*. Now Otter with difficulty managed to get a doctor, knowing this was a completely unnecessary ritual act. And the doctor did everything with extraordinary speed and indifference.

All the same, Otter still went to the pharmacist. Consciousness was fading. "Why aren't you asleep?" she would say to him in the middle of the day. And when he leant over the bed, she would avidly repeat: "Sleep, sleep," while Otter inwardly replied with something almost like mockery, of a painful sort: "Soon you'll fall asleep for ever." Her tongue had gone stiff. Her speech was unintelligible. She said: "Boo-boo." But then she suddenly said: "Let me give you a kiss." He felt lighter, as if with these words she was forgiving him his guilt, giving evidence that she would not carry away with her the insult and the bitterness. Was she aware? More than anything he feared she would be conscious. He tortured himself with doubts. Her face showed neither suffering nor exertion. He called her and in response

her eyelids jerked with a strange automatism. He clung to this link, and at the same time was afraid of those eyelids which responded to the sound of his voice. For this was consciousness, and perhaps there were thoughts, pre-death ones, which she could not now express. He stroked her forehead, kissed her. He heard her breathing at night. It was cold in the room, but after he had wrapped something round her head the breathing became calm. He still could not give up the stupid thought that the body had to be maintained and he kept on forcing warmed butter into her mouth (that same butter without bread and in lumps). Her mouth was closed, but two or three times she suddenly opened it wide with a kind of squeak. Yet their last conversation was nonetheless about food. In the evening he had pushed a small piece of sugar into her mouth. And asked, not at all relying on getting an answer: "Is it nice?" – when all of a sudden she replied very distinctly, like children pronouncing words they find difficult: "Of course. Give me another lump of sugar."

Nonetheless it is good that in her last days she had no appetite. That she did not die dreaming of an extra lump of sugar.

Her face was calm and serious. Under Otter's hand the brow went solemnly cold. Quite unlike her usual fussing appearance.

Otter feared for her any flashes of awareness. But was selfishly upset by her unconsciousness which prevented him from redeeming anything, receiving forgiveness or organizing her dying process. Everything happens swiftly. He knows that repentance felt once cannot be repeated. Both grief and repentance have now shrunk, are mere dummies, and the repentance is incommensurable with the size of the guilt. In the future Otter will go on punishing himself, forbidding himself relaxation and pleasure. He will go on being glad of domestic failures because she has escaped them, and grieving over achievements because she is not there; but all this is incommensurable.

All this was only a weak outline of the experiences bound to arise in that place.

But what changed straight away, unrestorably, was the function of food. In the last days he thought: "I'll go home, I'll see that everything's over, I'll eat all the bread, eat my fill, and after that there will still be the ration card." There was no strong sensation about this because Aunt had already gradually stopped eating, and he had gradually been eating more and more of what had been meant for two people. The fixed habit of bothering about food did not leave him. Chocolate and butter were issued. This was distressing as they were her favourites. From habit he was unwilling to forego gustatory sensations. She was lying there, dying. And he had concocted a sort of mixture of butter and chocolate and spread it on bread for her – and there was plenty of bread, more than ever before. He ate, and felt anguish. This was the sharpest feeling of anguish and grief that he felt in connection with this death. Food, the experiences of eating, were closely associated with her, and that was over now, and the interest – the human interest – of food was over; what remained was something dark and bestial. At the same time it seemed to him the anguish was being muffled by food, physically blocked by this nourishment, glued up by it as it went deep down there somewhere to meet the gnawing anguish. He chewed and swallowed, and the anguish came up in response. This was the saddest moment of all that he experienced in that time. He chewed and swallowed and the way of life, the lifestyle, that had been endured that year, was ending for him, with its "little joys", as Aunt used to say.

After that he was tortured by anguish and felt so unwell all the time that he continually wanted to change his position (as a person suffering from insomnia tosses about and keeps turning from side to side). He wanted to leave the room and go outdoors, for he thought movement would distract him. From outside he rushed back indoors, almost choking.

Then it seemed to him that the only possible position, the least painful one for him, was to sit at the table motionless and torpid, slowly rolling a cigarette. It did not help, and then it seemed to him he would feel easier if he went to see people he knew (with difficulty he must seek them out), or if he lay down in bed at last and stretched out, his face covered with a blanket – and this in fact helped him more than anything else.

Amongst all this there came a postcard from V in reply to his telegram. It was written with such overt sentimentality that it reached the level of shamelessness. From Otter's point of view the very fact of writing a postcard on such an occasion and in such a tone was shameless. V bluntly wrote: ". . . our beloved old lady, when I think that I shall never again see our darling . . ." That professional wit, that sceptic about ordinary life, and so on and so forth, was nonetheless not someone belonging to the intellectual culture which presupposes a unified world-view (or conscious dialectic of contradictions). It was precisely his professionalism that saved him from these problems. And he was abandoning the realms of serious and sensitive relations to things, realms in which he expressed himself absolutely primitively. "Our darling old lady, our beloved . . ." were, however, words he could surely not have spoken, being unaccustomed to such turns of speech. But he could write them, to satisfy a momentary emotional requirement.

Otter was not touched by this postcard. It caused him pain and made him angry. He was especially angered by the sentence that went: "I am to blame for something with regard to her, but I cannot sort this out at the moment." How lightly that lightweight person detached himself from an unavoidable feeling of guilt. In this, as in life generally, he always took the easy position. He lived for himself. Aunt had stayed with him as a guest; he sent money, and that only when it was not too difficult for him. He had not sorted the matter out at that moment, and of course he never would.

Because in a week's time there would no longer be any need for him to think about it. Having left Otter the whole physical stress of Aunt's existence, all the material privations and sufferings, he was now leaving him the whole burden of guilt and repentance as well. And those words, "beloved, darling old lady", sounded (if unintentionally) so very untrue; they were so terribly the opposite of the tragedy of evil, rudeness, bestial rage and everyday chaos which merged with the tragedy of her death, and which were what Otter had just endured, that Otter, as he read those words, groaned from pain. But that pain was certainly not one of tender emotion.

Speaking Directly About Life

Introduction to the 1995 Harvill edition

Lydia Ginzburg (1902–90), the celebrated literary scholar and author of *On Lyric Poetry*, *On Psychological Prose*, *On the Literary Hero*, as well as a whole series of learned articles on Russian literature, wrote essays and "notes" (*zapiski*) all her life. This material, however, perhaps the most significant part of her literary output, remained unknown to the reader for many years. Someone once said that in Russia you need to live long, in the sense that only longevity will enable you to see any change for the better in that country, and your most important works published. Indeed, it is only now, at the end of the eighties, that her essays have at length appeared, initially in journals, then in book form. *Person at a Writing Table* (1989) contained essays, memoirs and four narratives. One of these, *Notes from the Blockade*, can now be evaluated by the English reader. This piece was composed, one might say, in Hell: it is no coincidence that the name of the great Florentine surfaces on the page where she speaks of the fearful cold of the 1941–2 Leningrad winter.

Lydia Ginzburg's generation knew no rest: her childhood coincided with the first Russian revolution of 1905 and the First World War, her youth with the 1917 revolution and civil war, while her mature years were spent under the permanent threat of arrest, the concentration camp and the firing squad. To this should be added specific professional problems

and misfortunes. Lydia Ginzburg, whose teachers were brilliant critics and men of letters, like Yury Tynianov, Viktor Shklovsky, Boris Eikhenbaum and other representatives of the celebrated Formalist school of Russian criticism, was doomed, along with her mentors, to suffer the most savage criticism and persecution from official Soviet literary theory, at the behest of a directly interventionist party.

The fear of personal annihilation was ever-present, especially in 1937. Towards the end of 1952 also, the threat of death in Beria's torture-chambers loomed very close: at that time, in parallel with the "doctors' plot", the case of "Jewish sabotage in literary studies" was also in preparation. Only the death of the leader saved her from execution.

And on top of all came the 1941–5 war and the Leningrad Blockade, to which these memoirs are devoted.

A great deal has been written and published, both in Russia and the West, about the Leningrad Blockade. This includes not only official documents, articles, essays and statistics, not only memoirs and fictional narratives, but even poetry on every scale. The number of victims, as well as the reasons for their tragic destruction, reasons associated not only with the barbarity of the enemy, but with the incompetence and inhumanity of the Soviet leadership, had previously been distorted by the official version of the catastrophe. In Lydia Ginzburg's memoirs there are no statistical computations, no exposure of the party leadership – so why did it take more than forty years to see the light in the Gorbachev epoch?

I believe the explanation lies in a special quality of her prose – intellectualism. The intellectual heroes of the old literature had become obsolete, since "the new themes do not work with them" in the twentieth century. While they busied themselves resolving the "age-old" question of whether life is worth living – and then continued to live though denying life's meaning, individuals who have passed through the tragic school of the twentieth century have other concerns – the

daily struggle for their own personal dignity and the right to exist. "One possible way out . . . lies in calling upon the intellectual author to speak directly about life." That is precisely what takes place in Ginzburg's prose.

What does "blockade person" recall in the beleaguered city under bombardment? He recalls that in peacetime he used to listen to the sound of the ascending lift with a sinking heart: usually they came to arrest an individual at night. The Germans were also noted for punctuality, bombing at the same hour every day. There are many such fearful analogies and metaphors in the book. The starvation from which hundreds of thousands of people perished in blockaded Leningrad also had its "masks", its "psychological disguises". In a dystrophic daze, a man asks himself the question: "What is this so sickeningly like? What is it exactly like in my former life?" And perceives that it resembles an unhappy love affair – and also the endless humiliations to which Soviet existence has subjected him, one such humiliation being the vain hope of realizing one's creative potential in a totalitarian state.

The intellectual accommodation of suffering – that is the principal nerve running through this work. How can people live in a solitary cell, perform hard labour or exist in penury or humiliation, when their comfortably off contemporaries "in cosy cottages, put a bullet through their temple for no apparent reason?" Is it not because there is a process whereby suffering dislodges suffering, "the crazed driving urgency of the wretched", struggling to escape from the worst suffering (unbearable hunger, let's say) to a different one (cold or the terror of bombardment). "Suffering continually strives to be rid of itself, with the aid of a different, surrogate suffering."

The lofty intellectual intensity of prose like this manifests itself everywhere, even when analyzing the motifs of everyday conversation. "Self-assertion – that is the imperishable psychological essence of conversation!" So concludes the author, as she notes down the talk overheard in the

bread-queue during the blockade. Even a person living on the edge, the fine line between life and death, is prone to that same self-assertive urge. Tolstoy observed and revealed such things marvellously well, but never with such calamitous and distressing material.

Should we not reproach the author as heartless for being so coldly analytical? Try if you dare, if you do not shrink from comparing the comfortable situation of the reader of these records, biscuit or chocolate in hand, perhaps, with the icy chill of the blockade and the hunger spasms, which tormented the author of these memoirs in the course of her selfless analytical labour.

In a book about that fine Russian artist Mitrokhin, who also lived through the Leningrad Blockade, I came across a story told by a female friend of his. Encountering her in the street in the besieged city, the artist told her of his grim blockade existence, working in an unheated apartment, with his clothes ruinous and covered in mould. On parting, he asked her to come and do a bit of posing for him. "In this blue coat of yours, please," he added.

"That night, the instinct of trying to make sense of things and putting it into words held me back from despair. Thus does a person utilize his hurts, his griefs, even his emptiness, converting them all into grist for the mill," notes Lydia Ginzburg in 1931 in connection with the latest failure in her literary career, poisoned and defiled by the party's interference in literature. Ten years later, amid the ice and starvation of the blockade, she is saved from despair by that same creative effort.

What new thing did an individual learn about life, what was the value of this experience, the point of this unprecedented degradation and suffering? Or was what took place in Russia merely the play of chance, the mockery of history, a pointless absurdity?

In 1954, in one of her essays, Ginzburg gives her answer: "Talk of life being an empty and stupid joke is very much out of place, since contemporary existence offers all too many means for the ending of life, both personal and in the mass. Let us recall the life stories of our friends at least. Every one of them has had so many more opportunities of not existing than the opposite, that it is out of the question for him to speculate now on the vanity of existence."

In the twentieth century, she considers, "the age-old argument about the futility of life has come to an end, to be replaced by another – how to survive without losing one's human image." The realization of human solidarity, "the sense of the human nexus" – that is the countervailing force against individualism and helps people preserve their humanity in the cruellest of circumstances.

The word "nexus" is the key to understanding *Notes from the Blockade*. The proximate link of this social nexus was the family. "So painful, so fearful was it to touch one another, that in propinquity, at close quarters, it was hard to distinguish love from hatred – towards those one couldn't leave. One couldn't leave – but one *could* offend, hurt someone's pride. And so the nexus was maintained. . . . Writhing with pity, or cursing, people shared their bread. Cursing, they shared it, and sharing they died."

Notes from the Blockade is not for the faint-hearted, but English readers have travelled with Gulliver, they have experience of residence in upside-down worlds of fantasy. Nor should it be thought that the tragic Russian experience has no relevance to the westerner. It has. Because everything that is done on earth relates to each one of us, however distant we may be from the epicentre of historical disaster and suffering. Nor is it a matter of praise or blame whether we are born healthy or ailing, in the West or the East, in a prosperous country or a wretched one.

215

Any individual who has passed through the tragic ordeal of Russia – well of course not everyone, but the thinking person, a great rarity in any society – has discovered the worth of simple human pleasures: bread and central heating, piped water and sewerage, clean underwear and electric light, the "light-web" of sunbeams, ice-floes "rustling under bridges", "grainy granite", a child's sledge, stuck in a snow-drift, a Rembrandt canvas, "seaweed's false hair", "narrow, cunning wasps", a lake "standing sheer", "a dark-voiced violin bow" . . . He knows the value of these pleasures because he can picture only too well how speedily they can all be taken from him for ever. Only those who have not had to pay a high price for "the gentle joy of living and breathing" as Mandelstam puts it in one of his poems, can allow themselves feelings of melancholy, denial and lofty disdain for life. It was from those very poems of Mandelstam, written in the disastrous year of 1937, in anticipation of looming catastrophe, that I have borrowed this list of objects and phenomena. The more arbitrary the list, the more convincing it is, I do believe.

"It seems to me that modern art," says Ginzburg, "ought to speak of happiness and beauty. Because those two things are the reality of our experience and it is only this experience which gives a value to suffering and a dialectical meaning to negation . . . Misery gnawing on itself will never show a tragic flame."

The value of the tragic experience described by Ginzburg lies precisely in this awareness of everyday existence, in the affirmation of the possibility of happiness. That is our answer to God, if he exists, our "prayer of thankfulness". In this way, an unbeliever turns out to be religious in his attitude to life, his perception of its mysterious meaning – despite all the misfortunes that fall to his lot. People of a genuinely religious sensibility are marked by an inner spiritual gaiety, a joyous disposition in relation to other people

216

and new experiences, a confidence in life. Such were, no doubt, the Russian "elders" from the Optina Pustyn'*, such was Francis of Assisi.

It is wonderful that even a non-religious person, believing in history "because I know how it can remake minds", and in the mighty power of social mechanisms, which are capable of making "the supreme act of selflessness (symbolized in the redemptive sacrifice of Christ) into a paragraph of military regulations, intended for general use", can, as a result of comprehending the tragic experience of life, take on the same chaste and joyous attitude. "It would be absurd to declare that one should avoid unhappy people, but one should certainly steer clear of people who are unhappy on principle . . . It means more to me to talk with a happy person than with someone of high intelligence . . . It's terrible how easy it is to be unhappy; happiness, on the other hand, like anything fine, is only achieved with difficulty." I do love those words of hers.

I made Lydia Yakovlevna's acquaintance in 1959. I was still quite young then, and what struck me as so attractive was not just her analytical mind and tenacious memory, but the ability of a person of her age to react so ardently to poetry, to respond so gratefully to the seething rustle of the foliage outside the window, the scents of spring, the lambent white night of Leningrad. And also, of course, her wit (the notebooks are sprinkled with it), her trenchant views, her keen attention to psychological detail and minutiae. How could she, and those with whom she began her literary career, retain their interest in life to the very end? She could do it because life is not just a chronicle of suffering, but also a system of distractions from that, because it contains love, poetry, the beauties of nature

* A celebrated monastery in central Russia, founded in the fifteenth century. Noted in the nineteenth century as an institution, which interested Dostoevsky: that of tutorship of younger monks by older monks, called "elders" (*startsy*).

217

and, incidentally, humour. Lydia Yakovlevna knew what she was doing when she jotted in her notebook something which is not only very sad, but also very funny: "Akhmatova told Mandelstam once: 'Nobody complains, only you and Ovid complain'."

I should not like unknown readers of this book, gripped as they may be by the author's intellectual power, to picture her in their imagination as unsociable, or an ascetic recluse. Lydia Ginzburg was surrounded by people till the very last day; she loved friendly talk round the table, where, towards supper time, a decanter of vodka would invariably make its appearance. Thus it was that she invited my wife and me to visit her on the evening of 9 July 1990. That day, several hours before we were due to arrive, she suffered a stroke.

It was wonderful, all the same, that she witnessed the downfall of the system, lived long enough to see all the dizzying changes, receive the enthusiastic plaudits of new generations and read her published works (though there were one or two things she didn't release while she lived: mistrust and fear fostered by the long years of enforced silence still held sway). *Person at a Writing Table,* and the narrative *Notes from the Blockade,* like others of her works, tell more of the experience of life in twentieth-century Russia, than many multivolume novels or lengthy poems. If one does live in Russia, truly one needs to live long.

Alexander Kushner
St Petersburg, 1995

218

THE HISTORY OF VINTAGE

The famous American publisher Alfred A. Knopf (1892–1984) founded Vintage Books in the United States in 1954 as a paperback home for the authors published by his company. Vintage was launched in the United Kingdom in 1990 and works independently from the American imprint although both are part of the international publishing group, Random House.

Vintage in the United Kingdom was initially created to publish paperback editions of books bought by the prestigious literary hardback imprints in the Random House Group such as Jonathan Cape, Chatto & Windus, Hutchinson and later William Heinemann, Secker & Warburg and The Harvill Press. There are many Booker and Nobel Prize-winning authors on the Vintage list and the imprint publishes a huge variety of fiction and non-fiction. Over the years Vintage has expanded and the list now includes great authors of the past – who are published under the Vintage Classics imprint – as well as many of the most influential authors of the present. In 2012 Vintage Children's Classics was launched to include the much-loved authors of our youth.

For a full list of the books Vintage publishes,
please visit our website
www.vintage-books.co.uk

For book details and other information about the classic authors we publish, please visit the Vintage Classics website
www.vintage-classics.info